Airbnb Mortgage Loan Fundamentals

How Short-Term Rental Mortgage Loans Work and How to Qualify

By Joseph G. Correa

Licensed Mortgage Broker, Finibi Mortgage

Copyright & Legal Notice

Published by Live Stronger Faster

The information provided in this book is for educational and informational purposes only and should not be construed as financial, legal, or tax advice. Readers are encouraged to consult with licensed professionals before making any financial or real estate decisions. The author and publisher assume no responsibility for any losses or damages incurred as a result of the use or misuse of the information contained in this publication.

First Edition, 2026

Table of Contents

Foreword

The world of real estate investing has undergone a dramatic transformation in recent years, and at the center of that transformation is the rise of short-term rental platforms like Airbnb. What was once considered a niche strategy reserved for vacation homeowners and hospitality professionals has now evolved into one of the most powerful wealth-building tools available to modern investors. This shift has created an entirely new category of financing—Airbnb mortgage loans—designed specifically to support the acquisition, refinancing, and scaling of short-term rental properties. Book 1 of The Airbnb Mortgage Loan Mastery Series is your foundation for understanding this new landscape. It is designed to give you clarity, confidence, and a strategic advantage in a market where traditional rules no longer apply.

Unlike conventional real estate, Airbnb and short-term rental properties operate on a dynamic income model. Instead of fixed monthly rent, these properties generate revenue based on nightly rates, seasonal demand, occupancy trends, and guest experience. This variability introduces both opportunity and complexity. Traditional lenders, which rely heavily on predictable income streams and borrower employment verification, are often ill-equipped to evaluate these types of investments. As a result, a new class of loan products has emerged—designed specifically to assess the income potential of the property itself rather than the personal income of the borrower. Understanding how these loans work is the first step toward unlocking their full potential.

At its core, an Airbnb mortgage loan is not just a loan—it is a strategy. It represents a shift from borrower-based qualification to asset-based qualification. Instead of asking, "How much do you earn from your job?" lenders are increasingly asking, "How much can this property produce?" This fundamental shift opens the door for a wide range of investors who may not qualify under traditional guidelines. Self-employed individuals, entrepreneurs, digital nomads, and even beginners without extensive income documentation now have access to financing options that align with how they actually earn and invest.

One of the most important distinctions you will learn in this book is the difference between traditional mortgage loans, DSCR loans, and Non-QM (Non-Qualified Mortgage) loans. Traditional loans are designed for primary residences and long-term rental properties. They require full documentation, including tax returns, W-2s, and strict debt-to-income (DTI) ratios. While these loans often offer lower interest rates, they are limited in flexibility and scalability, especially for investors who want to grow quickly. In contrast, DSCR (Debt Service Coverage Ratio) loans represent a revolutionary approach to investment property financing. These loans focus on the income generated by the property itself. The DSCR ratio measures whether the rental income is sufficient to cover the mortgage payment. For Airbnb properties, this means lenders may evaluate projected short-term rental income using specialized data sources rather than relying solely on long-term lease comparisons. This opens up a powerful pathway for investors to qualify without traditional income verification, making it possible to scale faster and with fewer barriers.

Non-QM loans further expand the possibilities. These loans are designed for borrowers who fall outside conventional guidelines. They may include bank statement loans, asset-based loans, or hybrid programs that combine multiple forms of qualification. For Airbnb investors, Non-QM lending provides flexibility in structuring deals, especially when dealing with complex income profiles or unique property types. Understanding how to navigate these options—and when to use each one—is a key component of mastering Airbnb mortgage financing.

Another critical concept introduced in this book is the foundation of short-term rental income qualification. Unlike long-term rentals, where income is relatively stable and predictable, Airbnb income requires a more nuanced analysis. Factors such as average daily rate (ADR), occupancy rate, seasonality, local demand, and property management efficiency all play a role in determining income potential. Lenders may use tools such as AirDNA reports, market comparables, and appraiser-supported projections to estimate this income. As an investor, learning how to interpret and present this data can significantly improve your ability to qualify for financing and secure better terms.

Equally important is understanding who qualifies for Airbnb mortgage loans. One of the most exciting aspects of this financing model is its accessibility. You do not need to be a seasoned investor with a large portfolio to get started. Beginners can enter the market with the right strategy, especially when leveraging DSCR or low-documentation loan programs. Self-employed individuals, who often face challenges with traditional underwriting due to fluctuating income, can benefit greatly from asset-based and income-from-property approaches. Even high-income earners who prefer not to disclose extensive financial documentation may find these loans to be a more efficient and strategic option.

This book is designed to shift your mindset from limitation to possibility. Instead of asking whether you qualify under outdated rules, you will learn how to structure your profile and your deals to align with modern lending standards. You will begin to see financing not as a barrier, but as a tool—one that can be optimized, leveraged, and scaled. This shift in perspective is what separates casual investors from those who build substantial, income-generating portfolios.

As you progress through this series, you will move from foundational knowledge to advanced strategies. You will learn how to calculate DSCR using Airbnb-specific data, how to acquire your first property with minimal friction, how to scale multiple properties using portfolio strategies, and how to refinance and extract equity to fuel further growth. You will explore niche opportunities such as luxury Airbnb properties, vacation homes, and multi-unit investments. By the end of the series, you will have a comprehensive understanding of how to structure virtually any Airbnb deal using a combination of financing tools.

However, everything begins here—with a deep understanding of the fundamentals. This book lays the groundwork for everything that follows. It will help you understand the language of Airbnb lending, the logic behind underwriting decisions, and the strategic choices that determine whether a deal succeeds or fails. It will also prepare you to communicate effectively with lenders, brokers, and partners, positioning you as a knowledgeable and credible investor. The opportunity in short-term rentals is not just about owning property—it is about controlling income streams, leveraging data, and using financing strategically to accelerate growth. The investors who succeed in this space are not necessarily the ones with the most money or experience, but the ones who understand how to align opportunity with the right financing structure. That is what this series is designed to teach you.

As you begin this journey, remember that the goal is not just to learn how Airbnb mortgage loans work, but to master them. To see patterns where others see confusion. To identify opportunities where others see risk. And to build a system that allows you to finance, scale, and profit from short-term rental properties with clarity and confidence.

Welcome to Book 1: Airbnb Mortgage Loan Fundamentals. This is where your foundation is built, your strategy begins, and your path toward scalable, income-generating real estate truly starts.

Chapter 1

What Makes Airbnb Mortgage Loans Different

The evolution of real estate investing has always been tied closely to innovation, but few innovations have disrupted the industry as profoundly as short-term rental platforms like Airbnb. What once required hotel ownership, franchise agreements, or commercial real estate experience can now be executed by everyday individuals with the right property, the right strategy, and—most importantly—the right financing. This chapter is designed to break down what truly makes Airbnb mortgage loans different from traditional mortgage products, and why understanding these differences is essential if you want to succeed in the short-term rental space.

At the most basic level, the difference begins with how income is generated. Traditional real estate investing relies on long-term leases, typically spanning 6 to 12 months or longer. This creates predictable, stable income streams that lenders have historically relied upon to assess risk. In contrast, Airbnb properties operate on a nightly or short-term basis. Income fluctuates based on occupancy, pricing strategy, location demand, seasonality, and property quality. This creates a more dynamic income profile—one that can often outperform long-term rentals but is also more complex to analyze.

Because of this complexity, traditional mortgage guidelines were never designed to properly evaluate Airbnb income. A lender reviewing a standard loan application typically looks for W-2 income, tax returns, pay stubs, and a stable employment history. For investment properties, they may consider long-term lease agreements or appraised market rent. However, Airbnb income does not fit neatly into these categories. It may not show consistently on tax returns, especially if the property is newly acquired. It may vary significantly from month to month. And it often exceeds what a traditional rent analysis would suggest.

This gap between traditional underwriting and modern investment strategies led to the creation of specialized loan products, most notably DSCR loans and Non-QM loans. These loan types are designed to evaluate the performance of the asset rather than the personal income of the borrower. In other words, the property itself becomes the primary source of qualification. This is a fundamental shift that changes everything about how deals are structured.

With Airbnb mortgage loans, lenders are increasingly focused on one key question: can the property generate enough income to support the debt? This is where the concept of Debt Service

Coverage Ratio (DSCR) becomes critical. Instead of calculating a borrower's debt-to-income ratio based on personal earnings, DSCR measures the relationship between the property's income and its expenses, including the mortgage payment. If the property can cover its own costs—and ideally produce a surplus—the loan is considered less risky, regardless of the borrower's employment situation.

Another major difference lies in how income is estimated. For long-term rentals, appraisers typically use comparable rental properties in the area to determine market rent. For Airbnb properties, this approach is often insufficient. Instead, lenders may rely on specialized data sources such as short-term rental analytics platforms, historical booking data, or appraisals that include short-term rental projections. These tools analyze factors like average daily rate, occupancy rate, and seasonal demand to estimate potential income. This means that two identical properties in the same neighborhood could be valued very differently depending on their performance as short-term rentals.

The underwriting process itself also reflects these differences. Traditional loans are heavily documentation-driven. Borrowers must provide extensive financial records, and even minor inconsistencies can delay or derail the approval process. Airbnb mortgage loans, particularly DSCR and Non-QM loans, are often more flexible. While they still require documentation, the focus shifts toward property performance, credit profile, and reserves rather than detailed income verification. This can significantly streamline the approval process, especially for investors with non-traditional income sources.

Another important distinction is scalability. Traditional financing can become a bottleneck for investors who want to acquire multiple properties. Debt-to-income ratios increase with each new loan, eventually limiting borrowing capacity. Airbnb mortgage loans, on the other hand, allow investors to scale more efficiently because each property is evaluated independently. As long as each property meets the required DSCR threshold, investors can continue to expand their portfolio without being constrained by personal income limitations.

Risk perception also differs between traditional and Airbnb lending. From a lender's perspective, short-term rentals can appear riskier due to income variability and regulatory uncertainty. As a result, Airbnb mortgage loans may come with slightly higher interest rates, larger down payment requirements, or stricter reserve requirements. However, these perceived risks are often offset by the higher income potential of short-term rentals. For investors who understand how to optimize pricing, manage occupancy, and deliver exceptional guest experiences, the rewards can far exceed the costs.

Location plays an even more critical role in Airbnb financing than in traditional real estate. While location has always been important, short-term rentals are particularly sensitive to tourism demand, local regulations, and seasonal trends. A property in a high-demand vacation market may generate significantly more income than a similar property in a less desirable area. Lenders recognize this and may place greater emphasis on market data when evaluating Airbnb loans. This means that investors must not only understand financing but also conduct thorough market research to ensure their property aligns with lender expectations.

Another factor that sets Airbnb mortgage loans apart is the importance of property management strategy. Unlike long-term rentals, which can often be managed passively, Airbnb properties require active management. This includes listing optimization, pricing adjustments, guest communication, cleaning coordination, and maintenance. Lenders may consider whether a property will be professionally managed or self-managed, as this can impact income stability. A well-managed property is more likely to meet or exceed projected income, which strengthens the overall loan profile. Regulatory considerations also play a significant role. Many cities and municipalities have specific rules governing short-term rentals, including licensing requirements, zoning restrictions, and occupancy limits. These regulations can directly impact a property's ability to generate income. Lenders are increasingly aware of these factors and may require confirmation that the property complies with local laws. As an investor, understanding and navigating these regulations is just as important as securing financing.

Ultimately, what makes Airbnb mortgage loans different is not just the loan product itself, but the entire framework in which it operates. It represents a shift toward performance-based lending, where the success of the investment is tied directly to the property's ability to produce income. This creates a more entrepreneurial approach to real estate, where investors must think strategically about every aspect of the deal—from acquisition and financing to management and optimization.

As you move forward in this book and throughout the series, you will begin to see how these differences can be leveraged to your advantage. You will learn how to identify properties that align with lender criteria, how to structure deals that maximize approval chances, and how to position yourself as a low-risk, high-opportunity borrower. This knowledge will allow you to move beyond the limitations of traditional financing and into a more flexible, scalable, and profitable model. The key takeaway from this chapter is that Airbnb mortgage loans are not simply an alternative to traditional loans—they are a completely different way of thinking about real estate financing. They require a deeper understanding of market dynamics, income modeling, and strategic planning. But for those who are willing to learn and adapt, they offer a powerful pathway to building wealth through short-term rental investing.

Now that you understand what makes Airbnb mortgage loans different, the next step is to apply this knowledge in real-world scenarios. In the following example, you will see how these concepts come together in a practical investment case, illustrating how an Airbnb property can be analyzed, financed, and evaluated using the principles introduced in this chapter.

Analyzing an Airbnb Property Using DSCR and Short-Term Rental Data

Imagine an investor named Daniel who is looking to purchase his first Airbnb property in a popular vacation market. The property is listed at $400,000 and is located in an area with strong tourism demand, consistent year-round bookings, and favorable short-term rental regulations. Daniel's goal is to use a DSCR loan so that he can qualify based on the property's income rather than his personal income, as he is self-employed and prefers not to rely on tax returns. Daniel plans to put 20%

down, which amounts to $80,000. This leaves a loan amount of $320,000. The lender offers him an interest rate of 7.5% on a 30-year fixed loan. Based on these terms, Daniel's monthly principal and interest payment is approximately $2,237. In addition to this, he must account for property taxes, insurance, and maintenance reserves, which bring his total monthly housing expense to approximately $2,800.

Next, Daniel needs to determine whether the property will generate enough income to meet the lender's DSCR requirements. The lender requires a minimum DSCR of 1.20, meaning the property must generate at least 20% more income than its total monthly expenses. To estimate income, Daniel uses short-term rental data from a platform that analyzes Airbnb performance in the area.

The data shows that similar properties have an average daily rate of $220 and an average occupancy rate of 70%. To calculate monthly income, Daniel multiplies the average daily rate by the number of days in a month and then adjusts for occupancy. Using 30 days as a baseline, the gross monthly income is calculated as follows: $220 multiplied by 30 days equals $6,600 in potential revenue. Applying the 70% occupancy rate, the adjusted monthly income is $4,620.

From this amount, Daniel must subtract operating expenses,

including cleaning, utilities, management (if applicable), and platform fees. He estimates these costs to be approximately 25% of gross income, which equals $1,155. After expenses, the net operating income is $3,465 per month.

To calculate the DSCR, Daniel divides the net operating income by the total monthly housing expense. In this case, $3,465 divided by $2,800 results in a DSCR of approximately 1.24. This exceeds the lender's minimum requirement of 1.20, meaning the property qualifies based on its projected income.

This example illustrates how Airbnb mortgage loans rely on property performance rather than personal income. Even though Daniel may not meet traditional debt-to-income requirements, the strength of the property's income allows him to secure financing. It also highlights the importance of accurate income projections and expense management. Small changes in occupancy rate, pricing, or expenses can significantly impact DSCR and overall deal viability.

Now imagine Daniel improves the property's performance through better management, professional photography, and optimized pricing strategies. If he increases the average daily rate to $240 and occupancy to 75%, his monthly income rises to $5,400. After expenses, his net operating income increases to approximately $4,050. With the same housing expense of

$2,800, his DSCR improves to 1.45, making the deal even stronger. This demonstrates the power of active management in short-term rental investing. Unlike traditional rentals, where income is largely fixed, Airbnb properties offer the ability to increase revenue through strategic improvements. This not only enhances cash flow but also strengthens the investor's position when seeking additional financing in the future.

Through this example, you can see how the concepts introduced in this chapter—income variability, DSCR, property-based qualification, and strategic optimization—come together in a real-world scenario. As you continue through this series, you will build on this foundation, learning how to identify high-performing properties, structure deals for maximum approval, and scale your portfolio using advanced financing strategies.

Chapter 2

DSCR vs Traditional vs Non-QM Loans for Airbnb Properties

Understanding the differences between DSCR loans, traditional mortgage loans, and Non-QM loan products is one of the most important steps in mastering Airbnb financing. These three categories represent fundamentally different approaches to evaluating risk, qualifying borrowers, and structuring real estate deals. For short-term rental investors, choosing the right loan type can mean the difference between getting approved or denied, scaling quickly or getting stuck, and maximizing profits or leaving money on the table.

Traditional mortgage loans are the most widely recognized form of financing. These loans are typically backed by agencies such as Fannie Mae and Freddie Mac and are designed primarily for owner-occupied properties and long-term rental investments. The qualification process is heavily focused on the borrower's personal financial profile. Lenders evaluate income through W-2s, tax returns, and pay stubs. They calculate a debt-to-income ratio (DTI) to determine whether the borrower can afford the mortgage payments. Credit score, employment stability, and financial reserves all play a critical role in approval. While traditional loans offer some of the lowest interest rates in the market, they are not always well-suited for Airbnb investors. One of the biggest limitations is how income is treated. For investment properties, lenders typically use long-term lease agreements or appraised market rent to determine income. This often undervalues Airbnb properties, which can generate significantly higher income through short-term rentals. Additionally, traditional loans limit the number of financed properties an investor can have, making it difficult to scale a portfolio beyond a certain point.

Another challenge with traditional loans is documentation. Borrowers must provide extensive financial records, and any inconsistencies can delay or derail the process. For self-employed individuals, this can be especially difficult, as taxable income is often reduced through deductions. This means that even if an investor is financially successful, they may not appear qualified on paper. For Airbnb investors who rely on flexible income streams, this creates a major barrier.

In contrast, DSCR loans offer a completely different approach. Instead of focusing on the borrower's personal income, DSCR loans evaluate the income generated by the property itself. The key metric is the Debt Service Coverage Ratio, which measures whether the property's income is sufficient to cover its expenses. This allows investors to qualify based on the performance of the asset rather than their employment or tax returns.

For Airbnb properties, this is a game-changer. Lenders may use short-term rental data, including average daily rate, occupancy rate, and seasonal trends, to estimate income. This provides a more accurate representation of the property's earning potential. As long as the projected income meets the required DSCR threshold, the borrower can qualify—even without traditional income documentation.

DSCR loans also offer significant advantages in terms of scalability. Because each property is evaluated independently, investors are not limited by their personal debt-to-income ratio. This makes it possible to acquire multiple properties in a relatively short period of time, provided each deal meets the lender's criteria. For investors looking to build a portfolio of Airbnb properties, this flexibility is essential.

However, DSCR loans are not without trade-offs. Interest rates are typically higher than traditional loans, and down payment requirements may be larger, often ranging from 20% to 25%. Lenders may also require higher credit scores and more substantial cash reserves. Despite these requirements, many investors find that the increased flexibility and scalability outweigh the additional costs. Non-QM loans represent a broader category of financing options designed for borrowers who do not fit within traditional guidelines. These loans include bank statement loans, asset-based loans, and hybrid programs that combine different forms of qualification. For Airbnb investors, Non-QM loans provide an additional layer of flexibility, especially in complex scenarios.

Bank statement loans, for example, allow borrowers to qualify based on deposits into their bank accounts rather than tax returns. This is particularly useful for self-employed individuals who have strong cash flow but low taxable income. Asset-based loans, on the other hand, use the borrower's assets—such as investment accounts or retirement funds—to demonstrate the ability to repay the loan. These options can be combined with Airbnb income projections to create a comprehensive qualification strategy.

One of the key advantages of Non-QM loans is their adaptability. Lenders in this space often have more flexibility to structure deals based on the unique characteristics of the borrower and the property. This can include interest-only options, flexible documentation requirements, and customized underwriting guidelines. For Airbnb investors dealing with unique properties, mixed-use scenarios, or unconventional income streams, Non-QM lending can provide solutions that traditional and DSCR loans cannot. When comparing these three loan types, it is important to consider your investment goals. If you are purchasing a primary residence or a long-term rental and have strong, stable income, a traditional loan may offer the best terms. However, if your goal is to invest in Airbnb properties and scale a portfolio, DSCR loans are often the most effective option. For more complex situations, Non-QM loans can provide the flexibility needed to close deals that would otherwise be difficult to finance.

Another important consideration is how each loan type affects your long-term strategy. Traditional loans may offer lower rates, but they can limit your ability to acquire additional properties. DSCR loans may have higher rates, but they allow for faster scaling and greater flexibility. Non-QM loans may come with unique terms, but they can unlock opportunities that align with your specific financial profile.

It is also important to understand that these loan types are not mutually exclusive. Many successful investors use a combination of traditional, DSCR, and Non-QM loans to build and manage their portfolios. For example, an investor might use a traditional loan to purchase a primary residence, DSCR loans to acquire Airbnb properties, and Non-QM loans to refinance or access equity. By understanding how each loan type works, you can create a financing strategy that adapts to your needs and evolves with your portfolio. As the Airbnb market continues to grow, lenders are becoming more sophisticated in how they evaluate short-term rental properties. This means that the gap between traditional underwriting and modern investment strategies is narrowing. However, the core differences between DSCR, traditional, and Non-QM loans remain critical to understand. These differences shape how deals are structured, how properties are evaluated, and how investors scale their businesses.

The key takeaway from this chapter is that there is no one-size-fits-all approach to Airbnb financing. Each loan type has its strengths and limitations, and the best choice depends on your specific situation. By understanding these options, you can position yourself to take advantage of the opportunities in the short-term rental market while minimizing risk and maximizing flexibility.

Comparing DSCR, Traditional, and Non-QM Loan Scenarios for an Airbnb Property

Consider an investor named Maria who is evaluating the purchase of an Airbnb property priced at $500,000. She is deciding between three financing options: a traditional mortgage, a DSCR loan, and a Non-QM bank statement loan. Each option has different requirements, costs, and implications for her investment strategy. Maria plans to put 20% down, which equals $100,000, resulting in a loan amount of $400,000. Under a traditional loan, she qualifies with a

6.5% interest rate and a 30-year term. Her monthly principal and interest payment is approximately $2,528. Including taxes, insurance, and other expenses, her total monthly housing cost is about $3,200.

Under the traditional loan scenario, the lender evaluates Maria's personal income. Her monthly income is $8,000, and her existing debts total $2,000 per month. Adding the new mortgage payment brings her total monthly obligations to $5,200. Dividing this by her income results in a debt-to-income ratio of 65%, which exceeds the typical maximum of 43% to 50%. As a result, Maria does not qualify for the traditional loan, despite having a strong investment opportunity.

Next, Maria considers a DSCR loan. The lender offers a 7.75% interest rate, resulting in a monthly principal and interest payment of approximately $2,865. With taxes and insurance, her total monthly housing expense is $3,500. Instead of evaluating her personal income, the lender focuses on the property's projected rental income.

Using short-term rental data, Maria estimates an average daily rate of $250 and an occupancy rate of 70%. This results in gross monthly revenue of $5,250. After deducting 25% for operating expenses, her net operating income is $3,937.

Dividing this by her total housing expense of $3,500 results in a DSCR of 1.12. While this is close, it falls slightly below the lender's minimum requirement of 1.20.

Maria then explores ways to improve the property's performance. By optimizing pricing and enhancing the listing, she increases the average daily rate to $275 and occupancy to 75%. This raises her gross monthly revenue to $6,187. After expenses, her net operating income increases to $4,640. Dividing this by her housing expense results in a DSCR of 1.33, which meets the lender's requirement and allows her to qualify.

Finally, Maria evaluates a Non-QM bank statement loan. The lender offers an 8.25% interest rate, resulting in a monthly payment of approximately $3,050. Her total housing expense is $3,700. Instead of using tax returns, the lender reviews her bank statements and determines that her average monthly deposits are $10,000. After applying an expense factor of 50%, her qualifying income is $5,000 per month.

With total monthly obligations of $5,700 (including existing debts and the new mortgage), Maria's debt-to-income ratio is 114%, which would normally be unacceptable. However, because this is a Non-QM loan, the lender may allow exceptions based on strong reserves, credit score, and property performance. Combined with the Airbnb income potential, Maria is able to secure approval under this program.

This example highlights the flexibility and trade-offs of each loan type. The traditional loan offers the lowest rate but fails due to strict DTI requirements. The DSCR loan provides a property-based solution but requires strong income performance. The Non-QM loan offers flexibility but comes with higher costs and unique underwriting considerations.

By understanding these differences, Maria is able to choose the financing option that aligns with her goals and successfully acquire the property. This demonstrates the importance of evaluating multiple loan scenarios and structuring deals strategically to maximize approval and profitability.

Chapter 3

Short-Term Rental Income Qualification Basics

One of the most important shifts in modern real estate financing is the move from borrower-based qualification to property-based qualification, especially in the world of Airbnb and short-term rental investing. In this chapter, you will learn how lenders evaluate short-term rental income, how that income is calculated, what data sources are used, and how to position your deal to meet underwriting standards. Mastering this process is essential because your ability to qualify—and scale—depends largely on how well you understand and present income.

Unlike traditional rental properties, where income is based on fixed lease agreements, short-term rentals operate on a variable income model. This means that income is not guaranteed month-to-month and can fluctuate based on demand, seasonality, pricing strategy, competition, and management quality. Because of this variability, lenders cannot rely on standard rent schedules alone. Instead, they use a combination of projections, historical data, and third-party analytics to estimate income potential. The first key concept in short-term rental income qualification is gross revenue. This is the total income generated by the property before expenses. For Airbnb properties, gross revenue is typically calculated using the average daily rate (ADR) multiplied by the number of booked nights. To estimate this, lenders and investors look at occupancy rates, which represent the percentage of days the property is booked over a given period. These two variables—ADR and occupancy—form the foundation of income projections.

However, gross revenue alone is not sufficient for underwriting. Lenders are primarily concerned with net operating income (NOI), which accounts for expenses associated with running the property. These expenses can include cleaning fees, property management, utilities, maintenance, platform fees, insurance, and supplies. In many cases, lenders apply a standardized expense ratio, often between 20% and 30% of gross revenue, to estimate NOI. This conservative approach helps account for variability and ensures that the property can sustain its expenses over time.

Another important component is the data source used to support income projections. Lenders often rely on third-party platforms that specialize in short-term rental analytics. These platforms aggregate data from similar properties in the area and provide estimates for ADR, occupancy, and revenue. Some lenders may also accept appraisals that include short-term rental income projections, commonly referred to as a "short-term rental appraisal" or "STR appraisal." In certain cases, if the property has an established rental history, lenders may use actual income data from platforms like Airbnb or VRBO.

The credibility of your data plays a critical role in approval. If your projections are unrealistic or unsupported, lenders may adjust them downward or reject them entirely. This is why it is essential to use reliable data sources and present conservative, well-documented estimates. A strong income presentation not only improves your chances of approval but can also lead to better loan terms.

Seasonality is another factor that distinguishes short-term rental income from traditional rent. Many Airbnb markets experience fluctuations throughout the year, with peak seasons generating significantly higher income than off-peak periods. Lenders typically average income over a 12-month period to account for these variations. As an investor, understanding seasonal trends allows you to create more accurate projections and avoid overestimating income.

Occupancy rate is often one of the most scrutinized variables in underwriting. While it may be tempting to assume high occupancy, lenders prefer conservative estimates that reflect realistic market conditions. For example, an occupancy rate of 65% to 75% is often considered reasonable in many markets, depending on location and property type. Overestimating occupancy can lead to inflated income projections, which may not withstand underwriting review.

Average daily rate is equally important. This represents the average price per night that the property can command. ADR is influenced by factors such as location, property size, amenities, design, and competition. Properties with unique features or premium finishes may achieve higher ADRs, while standard properties may need to compete on price. Understanding how to position your property within the market can significantly impact your income potential.

Another layer of complexity comes from expense management. While lenders may use standardized expense ratios, your actual expenses can vary depending on how you manage the property. Self-managed properties may have lower costs but require more time and effort. Professionally managed properties may have higher costs but offer greater consistency and scalability. Regardless of your approach, controlling expenses is key to maximizing net income and improving your DSCR.

Lenders also consider reserves when evaluating short-term

rental loans. Because of income variability, they often require borrowers to have several months of mortgage payments in reserve. This provides a buffer in case of lower-than-expected income or unexpected expenses. Strong reserves can also strengthen your overall loan profile and increase your chances of approval.

Another important concept is the difference between projected income and stabilized income. Projected income is based on market data and assumptions, while stabilized income reflects the property's actual performance over time. New investors typically rely on projections, while experienced operators may be able to use historical data from existing properties. As you build your portfolio, having a track record of successful properties can enhance your credibility with lenders.

It is also important to understand how lenders view risk in short-term rental income. While Airbnb properties can generate higher income than long-term rentals, they are also perceived as more volatile. This is why lenders apply conservative assumptions and require higher DSCR thresholds. By presenting strong data, maintaining reserves, and demonstrating a clear management strategy, you can mitigate these perceived risks and position yourself as a reliable borrower.

Ultimately, short-term rental income qualification is both a science and an art. It requires a combination of data analysis, market understanding, and strategic presentation. The more you understand how lenders evaluate income, the better you can structure your deals to meet their criteria. This knowledge not only improves your chances of approval but also helps you identify properties that are truly profitable.

As you continue through this series, you will build on these fundamentals and learn how to optimize income, reduce expenses, and scale your portfolio. But everything starts with understanding how income is calculated and evaluated. This is the foundation of Airbnb financing, and mastering it will give you a significant advantage in the market.

Calculating Airbnb Income, Expenses, and DSCR for Qualification

Let's consider an investor named Alex who is analyzing a potential Airbnb property priced at $450,000 in a high-demand tourist area. Alex wants to determine whether the property will qualify for a DSCR loan and whether it will generate sufficient cash flow.

Alex plans to put 25% down, which equals $112,500, resulting in a loan amount of $337,500. The lender offers a 7.75% interest rate on a 30-year loan. This results in a monthly principal and interest payment of approximately $2,418. Adding taxes, insurance, and other fixed costs brings the total monthly housing expense to $3,000.

To estimate income, Alex researches comparable Airbnb properties in the area. The data shows an average daily rate of $230 and an occupancy rate of 68%. To calculate gross monthly revenue, Alex multiplies the ADR by the number of days in a month and then adjusts for occupancy. Using 30 days as a baseline, the potential monthly revenue is $6,900. Applying the 68% occupancy rate results in actual gross monthly revenue of $4,692.

Next, Alex estimates operating expenses. These include cleaning fees, utilities, maintenance, platform fees, and supplies. He estimates these costs at 25% of gross revenue, which equals $1,173. Subtracting this from the gross revenue results in a net operating income of $3,519.

To calculate the DSCR, Alex divides the net operating income by the total housing expense. In this case, $3,519 divided by $3,000 equals a DSCR of 1.17. This is slightly below the lender's minimum requirement of 1.20, meaning the property does not initially qualify.

Rather than abandoning the deal, Alex looks for ways to improve the numbers. He identifies opportunities to increase the average daily rate by enhancing the property's design, adding amenities, and optimizing the listing. By increasing the ADR to $250 and improving occupancy to 72%, the gross monthly revenue rises to $5,400. After expenses, the net operating income increases to $4,050.

With the same housing expense of $3,000, the DSCR becomes 1.35, which exceeds the lender's requirement. This demonstrates how small improvements in pricing and occupancy can significantly impact qualification and profitability.

Alex also considers the impact of reducing expenses. By self-managing the property and negotiating better cleaning rates, he reduces expenses to 22% of gross revenue. This further increases net operating income and improves DSCR, providing an additional margin of safety.

This example highlights the importance of accurate income projections, expense management, and strategic optimization. It shows how investors can actively influence their qualification by improving property performance. It also demonstrates the dynamic nature of Airbnb income, where multiple variables interact to determine overall profitability.

As you apply these concepts to your own deals, you will begin to see how data, strategy, and execution come together to create successful investments. Mastering short-term rental income qualification is not just about getting approved for a loan—it is about building a sustainable and scalable business.

Chapter 4

Who Qualifies for Airbnb Mortgage Loans (Investors, Beginners, and Self-Employed Borrowers)

One of the most powerful aspects of Airbnb mortgage financing is its accessibility. Unlike traditional lending models that often favor salaried employees with predictable income and long employment histories, Airbnb mortgage loans open the door to a much broader range of borrowers. This includes real estate investors, first-time buyers, entrepreneurs, and self-employed individuals. In this chapter, you will learn who qualifies for these loans, how lenders evaluate different borrower profiles, and how to position yourself—regardless of your background—to secure financing.

The traditional mortgage system was built around stability. Lenders historically prioritized borrowers with W-2 income, consistent paychecks, and low debt-to-income ratios. While this model works well for conventional homebuyers, it excludes a large portion of modern investors who generate income in non-traditional ways. Entrepreneurs, freelancers, business owners, and digital creators often have strong cash flow but limited taxable income due to deductions. As a result, they may struggle to qualify under traditional guidelines, even if they are financially capable.

Airbnb mortgage loans, particularly DSCR and Non-QM loans, address this gap by shifting the focus from the borrower's personal income to the performance of the property. This allows a wide range of individuals to qualify, including those who would otherwise be excluded. The key is understanding how lenders evaluate different borrower types and what criteria must be met.

Let's begin with real estate investors. Investors are the primary audience for Airbnb mortgage loans. These individuals are typically focused on acquiring income-producing properties and building a portfolio over time. Lenders view investors differently than primary residence buyers. Instead of focusing solely on personal income, they evaluate the investor's experience, credit profile, and ability to manage or oversee the property. For experienced investors with a track record of successful properties, this can lead to more favorable terms and greater flexibility.

However, experience is not always required. Beginners can also qualify for Airbnb mortgage loans, especially through DSCR programs. This is one of the most significant advantages of this financing model. A first-time investor does not need years of experience or a large portfolio to get started. As long as the property meets income requirements and the borrower has a reasonable credit score and sufficient down payment, approval is possible. This democratization of access has allowed many individuals to enter the real estate market and build wealth through short-term rentals.

For beginners, the key challenge is demonstrating that the property itself is a strong investment. Since there is no track record, lenders rely heavily on projected income and market data. This means that beginners must be diligent in selecting properties, analyzing data, and presenting a clear investment strategy. A well-prepared deal can overcome a lack of experience and position a beginner as a credible borrower.

Self-employed borrowers represent another major group that benefits from Airbnb mortgage loans. Traditional underwriting often penalizes self-employed individuals because their taxable income is reduced by business deductions. Even if a business generates significant revenue, the reported income may appear insufficient for loan qualification. This creates a disconnect between actual financial strength and perceived eligibility.

DSCR and Non-QM loans provide solutions to this problem. By focusing on property income or using alternative documentation such as bank statements, lenders can evaluate the true financial capacity of self-employed borrowers. This allows entrepreneurs to leverage their business success into real estate investments without being constrained by traditional documentation requirements.

Credit score remains an important factor across all borrower types. While Airbnb mortgage loans are more flexible than traditional loans, lenders still use credit scores to assess risk. A higher credit score can lead to better interest rates, lower down payment requirements, and more favorable terms. Most DSCR lenders require a minimum credit score in the range of 620 to 680, although stronger profiles may receive better pricing.

Down payment and reserves are also critical components of qualification. Because Airbnb properties are considered investment properties, lenders typically require a down payment of 20% to 25%. In addition, borrowers must demonstrate financial reserves, often equivalent to several months of mortgage payments. These reserves provide a safety net in case of income fluctuations or unexpected expenses. For beginners, having strong reserves can compensate for a lack of experience and strengthen the overall application.

Another factor that influences qualification is the borrower's intent and strategy. Lenders want to see that the borrower has a clear plan for managing the property. This includes decisions about self-management versus professional management, pricing strategy, and occupancy optimization. A well-defined plan not only improves the likelihood of approval but also increases the chances of long-term success.

It is also important to understand how lenders view risk across different borrower profiles. Experienced investors with strong credit and reserves are typically seen as lower risk, even if they have multiple properties. Beginners may be viewed as higher risk due to lack of experience, but this can be mitigated through strong property performance and financial stability. Self-employed borrowers may face additional scrutiny, but alternative documentation can address these concerns.

One of the most significant advantages of Airbnb mortgage loans is the ability to scale. For traditional borrowers, scaling is often limited by debt-to-income ratios. Each new loan increases the borrower's obligations, eventually reaching a point where additional financing is no longer possible. With DSCR loans, each property is evaluated independently, allowing investors to continue acquiring properties as long as each deal meets the required criteria. This creates a pathway for rapid portfolio growth.

Another consideration is the type of entity used for ownership. Many investors choose to purchase Airbnb properties under an LLC or other business structure. This can provide liability protection and potential tax advantages. Some lenders allow DSCR loans to be issued to business entities, while others require the borrower to qualify personally. Understanding these requirements can help you structure your investments more effectively.

Geographic location and property type also influence qualification. Lenders may have specific guidelines for properties in certain markets, particularly those with strict short-term rental regulations. Additionally, unique property types such as cabins, beachfront homes, or luxury properties may require specialized underwriting. As an investor, selecting properties that align with lender guidelines can simplify the approval process.

Ultimately, the question of who qualifies for Airbnb mortgage loans is not limited to a specific demographic. It is a question of alignment—between the borrower, the property, and the lender's criteria. Whether you are an experienced investor, a beginner, or a self-employed entrepreneur, the key is to understand how your profile fits within this framework and how to position yourself accordingly.

The takeaway from this chapter is that Airbnb financing is more inclusive than traditional lending, but it still requires preparation and strategy. By understanding the requirements, strengthening your profile, and selecting the right properties, you can position yourself to qualify and succeed in this space. This knowledge empowers you to move forward with confidence, knowing that your background does not limit your potential.

Comparing Qualification Scenarios for an Investor, Beginner, and Self-Employed Borrower

Let's examine three different borrowers—an experienced investor, a beginner, and a self-employed entrepreneur—each attempting to purchase the same Airbnb property priced at $480,000. This example will illustrate how qualification varies based on borrower profile and loan type.

All three borrowers plan to put 25% down, which equals $120,000, resulting in a loan amount of $360,000. The DSCR loan offered has a 7.75% interest rate, with a monthly principal and interest payment of approximately $2,578. Including taxes and insurance, the total monthly housing expense is $3,200.

The property is located in a strong Airbnb market with an average daily rate of $240 and an occupancy rate of 70%. This results in gross monthly revenue of $5,040. After deducting

25% for expenses, the net operating income is $3,780. Dividing this by the housing expense results in a DSCR of 1.18, which is slightly below the lender's requirement of 1.20.

First, consider the experienced investor. This borrower has a credit score of 740, significant reserves, and a portfolio of successful Airbnb properties. Because of this track record, the lender is willing to make slight adjustments to the income projections, recognizing the investor's ability to optimize performance. By increasing the projected occupancy to 72% based on historical performance, the net operating income rises to $3,888, resulting in a DSCR of 1.21. This allows the investor to qualify.

Next, consider the beginner. This borrower has a credit score of 700, limited reserves, and no prior experience. The lender relies strictly on conservative projections and does not adjust the numbers. With a DSCR of 1.18, the deal initially does not qualify. However, the beginner improves the deal by increasing the down payment to 30%, reducing the loan amount to $336,000. This lowers the monthly housing expense to $3,000. With the same net operating income of $3,780, the DSCR becomes 1.26, allowing the borrower to qualify.

Finally, consider the self-employed borrower. This individual has a credit score of 720 and strong cash flow but low taxable income. Instead of relying on personal income, the borrower uses a DSCR loan combined with bank statement verification. The lender reviews 12 months of bank statements and confirms consistent deposits. Combined with the property's income potential, the borrower is approved despite not meeting traditional income requirements.

This example demonstrates how different borrower profiles can achieve qualification through strategic adjustments. The experienced investor leverages expertise, the beginner increases the down payment, and the self-employed borrower uses alternative documentation. In each case, understanding the lender's criteria and adapting the strategy leads to a successful outcome.

As you move forward, consider your own profile and how it aligns with these scenarios. By identifying your strengths and addressing potential weaknesses, you can position yourself to qualify for Airbnb mortgage loans and begin building your portfolio with confidence.

Chapter 5

Structuring Your First Airbnb Deal for Approval and Profit

Securing an Airbnb mortgage loan is not just about finding a lender—it is about structuring a deal that aligns perfectly with underwriting guidelines while also maximizing profitability. Many investors focus heavily on finding the "perfect property," but overlook the importance of deal structure. In reality, how you structure your deal—your purchase price, down payment, loan type, income projections, and expense management—often determines whether you get approved and whether the investment performs as expected. This chapter is designed to help you think like both an investor and an underwriter, so you can build deals that work on paper and in real life.

The first step in structuring your Airbnb deal is understanding that lenders and investors look at the same numbers differently. As an investor, your primary goal is to maximize cash flow and long-term appreciation. As a lender, the goal is to minimize risk and ensure that the property can support the debt. The key to success is aligning these two perspectives. When a deal is structured properly, it not only generates strong returns but also meets or exceeds lender requirements, making approval much easier. Everything begins with the purchase price. The price you pay for a property directly impacts your loan amount, monthly payment, and overall profitability. Overpaying—even slightly—can reduce your DSCR and make it difficult to qualify. On the other hand, negotiating a better purchase price or finding undervalued properties can significantly improve your numbers. Successful investors understand that profit is made at the time of purchase, not just through operations.

The next critical component is the down payment. Most Airbnb mortgage loans require a down payment of 20% to 25%, but increasing your down payment can dramatically improve your deal structure. A larger down payment reduces your loan amount, lowers your monthly payment, and improves your DSCR. While this requires more upfront capital, it can be the difference between a deal that qualifies and one that does not. It also provides a cushion that reduces risk and increases long-term stability.

Loan selection is another key factor. Choosing between a DSCR loan, a Non-QM loan, or a hybrid structure depends on your financial profile and investment goals. For most Airbnb investors, DSCR loans offer the best balance between flexibility and scalability. However, understanding the terms of your loan—interest rate, amortization period, prepayment penalties, and reserve requirements—is essential. A slightly higher interest rate may be acceptable if it allows you to scale faster or qualify more easily.

Income projection is where many deals succeed or fail. As discussed in previous chapters, lenders rely on projected income based on average daily rate and occupancy. However, not all projections are created equal. Conservative, well-supported projections are far more likely to be accepted than overly optimistic estimates. Using reliable data sources and aligning your projections with market trends can strengthen your application and improve your credibility with lenders.

At the same time, you should be thinking beyond qualification and focusing on optimization. How can you increase your average daily rate? How can you improve occupancy? What amenities or design features can set your property apart from competitors? These are not just operational questions—they are financial ones. Small improvements in performance can significantly increase your net operating income and overall return on investment.

Expense management is equally important. Many new investors underestimate the costs associated with running an Airbnb property. Cleaning fees, utilities, maintenance, platform fees, and supplies can add up quickly. Lenders often assume a standardized expense ratio, but your actual expenses may vary. By managing these costs effectively, you can improve your net income and strengthen your DSCR. This not only helps with loan approval but also increases your profitability.

Another important aspect of deal structuring is reserves. Lenders typically require several months of mortgage payments in reserve, but having additional reserves can provide a strategic advantage. It allows you to weather periods of lower occupancy, invest in property improvements, and take advantage of new opportunities. Strong reserves also signal to lenders that you are financially prepared, which can improve your chances of approval.

One of the most overlooked elements of structuring an Airbnb deal is exit strategy. While the focus is often on acquisition and operation, you should also consider how you will refinance, sell, or leverage the property in the future. A well-structured deal provides flexibility, allowing you to adapt to changing market conditions. Whether your goal is to hold long-term, refinance to extract equity, or sell for a profit, your initial structure should support that strategy.

Market selection also plays a critical role in deal structuring. Not all markets are equally suited for Airbnb investments. Factors such as tourism demand, local regulations, competition, and seasonality all impact income potential. Choosing the right market can enhance your projections, improve your DSCR, and increase your chances of approval. It also reduces risk and improves long-term performance.

Another key consideration is property type. Single-family homes, condos, multi-unit properties, and unique listings such as cabins or luxury homes each have different income potential and risk profiles. Lenders may have specific guidelines for certain property types, so understanding these requirements can help you select properties that align with financing criteria.

Structuring your first Airbnb deal also requires a shift in mindset. Instead of asking, “Can I afford this property?” you should be asking, “Does this property qualify and perform?” This shift moves the focus from personal finances to investment performance. It allows you to think like a business owner, where each property is a standalone asset that must justify its own existence.

Another important strategy is layering strengths within your deal. If one aspect of your profile is weaker—such as limited experience—you can compensate with stronger elements, such as a larger down payment, higher reserves, or a stronger property. This holistic approach allows you to overcome potential obstacles and present a well-rounded application. It is also important to build relationships with lenders and brokers who specialize in Airbnb financing. These professionals understand the nuances of short-term rental underwriting and can guide you through the process. They can also help you identify opportunities, structure deals, and navigate challenges. Having the right team in place can significantly improve your chances of success.

Ultimately, structuring your first Airbnb deal is about creating alignment. Alignment between the property and the market, between the income and the expenses, and between your goals and the lender's requirements. When these elements come together, the result is a deal that not only gets approved but also generates strong returns.

The goal is not just to close one deal, but to create a repeatable system. By understanding how to structure deals effectively, you can replicate your success and build a portfolio of income-producing properties. This is the foundation of scalable real estate investing, and it begins with your first deal.

Structuring an Airbnb Deal for Approval and Maximum Profit

Let's walk through a detailed example of how to structure an Airbnb deal for both approval and profitability. Consider an investor named Jason who is evaluating a property priced at $420,000 in a high-demand vacation market. Jason initially plans to put 20% down, which equals $84,000, resulting in a loan amount of $336,000. The lender offers a DSCR loan at a 7.75% interest rate. This results in a monthly principal and interest payment of approximately $2,406. Adding taxes, insurance, and other costs brings the total monthly housing expense to $3,000.

Jason researches comparable Airbnb properties and finds that the average daily rate is $230 with an occupancy rate of 68%. This results in gross monthly revenue of $4,692. After deducting 25% for expenses, the net operating income is $3,519. Dividing this by the housing expense results in a DSCR of 1.17, which is below the required 1.20.

At this point, the deal does not qualify. Instead of abandoning it, Jason begins restructuring.

First, he negotiates the purchase price down to $400,000. With the same 20% down payment, his loan amount decreases to $320,000. This reduces his monthly housing expense to approximately $2,850.

Next, Jason increases his down payment to 25%, which equals $100,000. This further reduces the loan amount to $300,000 and lowers the monthly housing expense to $2,650.

Now, Jason focuses on income optimization. By upgrading the property with modern furnishings, adding amenities such as a hot tub, and improving the listing with professional photography, he increases the average daily rate to $250 and occupancy to 72%. This results in gross monthly revenue of $5,400. After expenses, the net operating income increases to $4,050.

With a housing expense of $2,650, the DSCR is now 1.53, well above the lender's requirement. The deal not only qualifies but also provides a strong margin of safety.

Jason also looks at cash flow. With net operating income of $4,050 and housing expenses of $2,650, his monthly cash flow is $1,400. Over a year, this equates to $16,800 in cash flow.

Finally, Jason considers his return on investment. With a total cash investment of $100,000 (down payment) plus $20,000 in renovations and reserves, his total investment is $120,000.

With annual cash flow of $16,800, his cash-on-cash return is 14%.

This example illustrates how structuring a deal can transform it from a marginal investment into a highly profitable one. By adjusting the purchase price, down payment, and income strategy, Jason improves both qualification and performance.

It also demonstrates the importance of taking a proactive approach. Instead of accepting initial numbers at face value, successful investors look for ways to improve every aspect of the deal. This mindset allows them to consistently identify opportunities, secure financing, and build profitable portfolios.

As you begin structuring your own deals, remember that every variable matters. Small changes in price, financing, or performance can have a significant impact on your results. By mastering this process, you can position yourself for long-term success in the Airbnb investment space.

Chapter 6

Risk, Regulations, and Long-Term Sustainability in Airbnb Financing

As you move deeper into Airbnb investing and financing, it becomes increasingly important to understand not just how to get approved for a loan, but how to sustain and protect your investment over time. Many new investors focus heavily on income potential and loan approval, but overlook the risks that can impact long-term success. In this chapter, you will learn how lenders and investors evaluate risk, how regulations affect your ability to operate, and how to build a sustainable Airbnb business that can withstand market changes.

Risk in Airbnb investing is fundamentally different from traditional real estate risk. In long-term rentals, risk is often tied to tenant stability and lease agreements. Once a tenant is in place, income is relatively predictable. In contrast, Airbnb properties operate in a dynamic environment where income is influenced by multiple variables. These include occupancy fluctuations, seasonal demand, competition, pricing strategy, and guest experience. This variability introduces both opportunity and uncertainty. From a lender's perspective, the primary concern is whether the property can consistently generate enough income to cover its debt obligations. This is why DSCR requirements are typically set above 1.0, often around 1.20 or higher. This buffer is designed to account for potential income fluctuations. As an investor, your goal should be to exceed this minimum threshold by a comfortable margin, creating a cushion that protects your investment during slower periods.

One of the most significant risks in Airbnb investing is income volatility. Even in strong markets, occupancy and pricing can vary throughout the year. Peak seasons may generate substantial income, while off-peak periods may see reduced bookings. Understanding these patterns is essential for accurate projections and financial planning. Investors who rely on peak-season income to justify a deal may find themselves struggling during slower months.

Another important risk factor is competition. As more investors enter the short-term rental market, competition increases. This can lead to downward pressure on pricing and occupancy. Properties that stand out through design, amenities, and guest experience are more likely to maintain strong performance. Continuous improvement and market awareness are key to staying competitive.

Operational risk is another consideration. Managing an Airbnb property requires attention to detail, responsiveness, and consistency. Poor management can lead to negative reviews, reduced bookings, and lower income. Whether you choose to self-manage or hire a professional management company, having a reliable system in place is essential. Lenders may also consider management strategy when evaluating risk, as professionally managed properties often demonstrate more stable performance.

Regulations represent one of the most critical—and often overlooked—factors in Airbnb investing. Many cities and municipalities have implemented rules governing short-term rentals. These regulations can include licensing requirements, zoning restrictions, occupancy limits, and even outright bans in certain areas. Failing to comply with these regulations can result in fines, legal issues, or the inability to operate the property as intended.

Before purchasing an Airbnb property, it is essential to research local regulations thoroughly. This includes understanding whether short-term rentals are permitted, what permits are required, and any restrictions on usage. Some markets may allow short-term rentals only in certain zones or under specific conditions. Others may require the property to be owner-occupied or limit the number of rental days per year. Lenders are increasingly aware of regulatory risk and may require confirmation that the property complies with local laws. In some cases, they may restrict lending in areas with uncertain or restrictive regulations. As an investor, choosing markets with stable and favorable regulatory environments can significantly reduce risk and improve long-term viability.

Another layer of risk comes from economic conditions. Changes in the economy can impact travel demand, which in turn affects Airbnb income. During economic downturns, discretionary travel may decline, leading to lower occupancy rates. However, some markets may remain resilient due to consistent demand from business travel, events, or essential tourism. Diversifying your portfolio across different markets can help mitigate this risk.

Interest rate risk is also an important consideration. Many Airbnb loans come with higher interest rates than traditional mortgages, and some may include adjustable-rate features. Changes in interest rates can impact your monthly payments and overall profitability. Understanding your loan terms and planning for potential rate changes is essential for long-term stability.

Insurance and liability are additional factors that contribute to risk. Airbnb properties may require specialized insurance policies that cover short-term rental activity. Standard homeowner's insurance may not provide adequate coverage.

Ensuring that your property is properly insured protects you from potential losses related to damage, liability claims, or unforeseen events.

Another critical concept is the importance of reserves. Having sufficient cash reserves allows you to manage periods of lower income, unexpected expenses, or market disruptions. Lenders typically require a minimum level of reserves, but experienced investors often maintain additional funds to provide greater flexibility and security. Strong reserves can mean the difference between weathering a downturn and being forced to sell prematurely.

Sustainability in Airbnb investing is not just about surviving risks—it is about building a system that can adapt and grow over time. This includes continuously monitoring market trends, adjusting pricing strategies, upgrading properties, and optimizing operations. Investors who treat their Airbnb properties as active businesses rather than passive investments are more likely to achieve long-term success.

Another key aspect of sustainability is scalability. As you acquire more properties, managing risk becomes even more important. Each additional property introduces new variables and potential challenges. Developing standardized processes, leveraging technology, and building a reliable team can help you manage a growing portfolio effectively.

It is also important to consider exit strategies as part of your long-term plan. Whether you plan to refinance, sell, or transition properties to long-term rentals, having a clear exit strategy provides flexibility. Market conditions can change, and being able to adapt your strategy ensures that you can protect your investment and capitalize on opportunities.

Ultimately, successful Airbnb investing requires a balance between opportunity and risk management. While the income potential of short-term rentals is attractive, it must be supported by a solid foundation of planning, compliance, and financial discipline. By understanding the risks and proactively addressing them, you can create a sustainable investment model that generates consistent income and long-term growth.

The key takeaway from this chapter is that risk is not something to be avoided—it is something to be managed. With the right knowledge, strategies, and mindset, you can navigate the complexities of Airbnb investing and build a resilient, profitable portfolio.

Stress Testing an Airbnb Investment for Risk and Sustainability

Let's analyze a real-life scenario where an investor named Sophia purchases an Airbnb property for $500,000 in a popular vacation market. Sophia puts 25% down ($125,000), resulting in a loan amount of $375,000. She secures a DSCR loan at a 7.75% interest rate, with a monthly principal and interest payment of approximately $2,685. Including taxes, insurance, and other expenses, her total monthly housing cost is $3,400.

Based on market data, the property has an average daily rate of $260 and an occupancy rate of 72%. This results in gross monthly revenue of $5,616. After deducting 25% for operating expenses ($1,404), her net operating income is $4,212. Dividing this by her housing expense results in a DSCR of 1.24, which meets the lender's requirement.

At first glance, the deal appears solid. However, Sophia decides to stress test the investment to evaluate its sustainability under different scenarios.

First, she considers a downturn in occupancy. If occupancy drops from 72% to 60%, her gross monthly revenue decreases to $4,680. After expenses, her net operating income becomes $3,510. With a housing expense of $3,400, her DSCR drops to 1.03. While still above 1.0, this leaves very little margin for error.

Next, Sophia analyzes the impact of increased competition, which forces her to lower her average daily rate from $260 to

$230. With the original 72% occupancy, her gross monthly revenue becomes $4,968. After expenses, her net operating income is $3,726. This results in a DSCR of 1.10, which is below the lender's preferred threshold.

Sophia then evaluates a combined scenario where both occupancy and ADR decrease. With a $230 ADR and 60% occupancy, her gross monthly revenue drops to $4,140. After expenses, her net operating income is $3,105. This results in a DSCR of 0.91, meaning the property no longer covers its debt obligations.

To mitigate these risks, Sophia builds a reserve fund equal to six months of mortgage payments, totaling approximately $20,400. This provides a financial cushion that allows her to manage temporary declines in income.

She also invests in property improvements to increase competitiveness, including upgraded furnishings, enhanced amenities, and professional marketing. These improvements help maintain higher occupancy and pricing, even in competitive markets.

Additionally, Sophia diversifies her strategy by targeting both short-term and mid-term rentals, allowing her to adjust her approach based on market conditions. This flexibility reduces her reliance on peak-season income and improves overall stability. Finally, Sophia monitors local regulations and ensures compliance with all requirements, reducing the risk of operational disruptions.

This example demonstrates the importance of stress testing and proactive risk management. By analyzing different scenarios and preparing for potential challenges, Sophia transforms a good deal into a sustainable investment. It highlights that success in Airbnb investing is not just about maximizing income, but about building resilience and adaptability into your strategy.

As you apply these principles to your own investments, remember that the goal is not just to qualify for a loan, but to create a long-term, sustainable business. By understanding and managing risk, you can protect your investments and position yourself for continued growth in the Airbnb market.

Chapter 7

Building a Scalable Airbnb Portfolio Using Smart Financing Strategies

Once you understand how to qualify for Airbnb mortgage loans and structure a profitable deal, the next step is scaling. This is where real wealth is built—not from owning one property, but from controlling multiple income-producing assets that work together as a system. In this chapter, you will learn how to transition from a single Airbnb investment to a scalable portfolio using smart financing strategies, leverage, and disciplined execution.

Scaling begins with a mindset shift. Your first deal is not the end goal—it is the foundation. Many investors stop after acquiring one property because they focus only on immediate cash flow or fear taking on additional risk. However, successful investors view each property as a stepping stone. The goal is to create a repeatable process that allows you to acquire, stabilize, and leverage properties over time.

One of the most powerful tools for scaling is leverage. In real estate, leverage allows you to control large assets with relatively small amounts of capital. By using financing strategically, you can acquire multiple properties without needing to pay cash for each one. Airbnb mortgage loans, particularly DSCR loans, are designed to support this approach because they evaluate each property independently based on its income.

The key to scaling is ensuring that each property meets or exceeds lender requirements. This means maintaining strong DSCR ratios, managing expenses effectively, and optimizing income. When each property performs well, it becomes easier to qualify for additional loans. This creates a compounding effect, where each successful deal enables the next.

Another important strategy is recycling capital. Instead of leaving your equity locked in a property, you can refinance or use cash-out strategies to access that equity and reinvest it into new properties. This approach allows you to grow your portfolio without constantly injecting new capital. Understanding when and how to refinance is critical for long-term scaling.

The BRRRR strategy—Buy, Rehab, Rent, Refinance, Repeat—is commonly used in long-term rentals, but it can also be adapted for Airbnb investing. In this model, you purchase a property below market value, improve it to increase income potential, stabilize its performance, and then refinance based on the higher value and income. The funds from the refinance can then be used for your next acquisition. Portfolio diversification is another key element of scaling. Relying on a single property or market increases risk. By investing in different locations, property types, and price points, you can reduce exposure to market-specific risks. For example, a beach property may perform well in summer, while a city property may have consistent year-round demand. Diversification creates balance and stability within your portfolio.

As your portfolio grows, efficiency becomes increasingly important. Managing multiple properties requires systems and processes that can handle increased complexity. This includes booking management, pricing optimization, cleaning coordination, and maintenance. Many investors leverage technology and automation tools to streamline operations. Others hire property management companies to handle day-to-day tasks.

Financing strategy also evolves as you scale. While your first property may require conservative structuring, subsequent deals can be approached more strategically. You may combine different loan types, use cross-collateralization, or leverage existing assets to secure better terms. Building relationships with lenders who understand your portfolio can also lead to more flexible and favorable financing options.

Another critical factor in scaling is maintaining strong financial discipline. It can be tempting to expand quickly, but over-leveraging can create significant risk. Each new property should be evaluated carefully to ensure it contributes positively to your portfolio. Maintaining healthy cash flow, reserves, and DSCR ratios across all properties is essential for long-term success.

Credit management plays a significant role as well. A strong credit profile allows you to access better loan terms and more financing options. As you scale, it is important to monitor your credit, manage debt responsibly, and avoid unnecessary risks that could impact your ability to secure future loans.

Tax strategy is another consideration when building a portfolio. Owning multiple Airbnb properties can create opportunities for tax optimization, including deductions, depreciation, and entity structuring. Working with a knowledgeable tax professional can help you maximize these benefits and improve your overall returns.

Market timing and opportunity recognition are also important. Not every deal will be ideal for scaling. Successful investors are patient and selective, focusing on properties that align with their long-term strategy. This may mean waiting for the right opportunity rather than rushing into a deal that does not meet your criteria.

Another important concept is the snowball effect of scaling. As your portfolio grows, your income increases, your equity builds, and your access to financing improves. This creates momentum that accelerates growth. Each property contributes to a larger system that becomes increasingly efficient and profitable over time.

However, scaling is not without challenges. Managing multiple properties, navigating regulations, and maintaining performance across a portfolio requires discipline and adaptability. Investors who succeed in scaling are those who treat their portfolio as a business, continuously refining their strategy and improving their operations.

Long-term vision is essential. Scaling is not just about acquiring properties—it is about building a sustainable, income-generating system that can support your financial goals. Whether your objective is financial independence, passive income, or generational wealth, your portfolio should be structured to align with that vision.

Another advanced strategy involves layering financing options. For example, you might use DSCR loans for acquisitions, Non-QM loans for refinances, and traditional loans for primary residences or lower-risk properties. This layered approach allows you to optimize each deal based on its specific characteristics. As you scale, your focus should shift from individual deals to portfolio performance. This means analyzing metrics such as overall cash flow, average DSCR, occupancy trends, and return on investment across all properties. This broader perspective helps you make strategic decisions that enhance the entire portfolio.

Ultimately, building a scalable Airbnb portfolio is about creating a system that works. It is about combining smart financing, disciplined investing, and effective management to achieve consistent growth. The strategies outlined in this chapter provide a roadmap for moving beyond your first deal and building a portfolio that generates long-term wealth.

Scaling from One Airbnb Property to a Five-Property Portfolio

Let's follow an investor named Ryan as he scales his Airbnb portfolio from one property to five using smart financing strategies.

Ryan begins with his first property, purchased for $400,000. He puts 25% down ($100,000) and secures a DSCR loan for $300,000 at a 7.75% interest rate. His total monthly housing expense is $2,800. The property generates net operating income of $4,200, resulting in a DSCR of 1.50 and monthly cash flow of $1,400.

After one year, the property appreciates to $440,000 due to market growth and improved performance. Ryan refinances at 75% loan-to-value, resulting in a new loan of $330,000. After paying off the original loan, he pulls out $30,000 in equity.

Ryan combines this $30,000 with $70,000 in savings to purchase a second property for $400,000. This property performs similarly, generating $1,300 in monthly cash flow.

Now with two properties, Ryan's total monthly cash flow is $2,700.

He repeats this process, refinancing his second property after appreciation and using the equity to fund a third purchase. By the time he acquires his third property, his total portfolio cash flow increases to approximately $4,000 per month.

As Ryan continues, he becomes more efficient in identifying deals and optimizing performance. His fourth and fifth properties benefit from improved strategies, generating higher income and stronger DSCR ratios.

By the time Ryan owns five properties, each generating an average of $1,300 per month, his total monthly cash flow reaches $6,500, or $78,000 annually.

His total invested capital across all properties is approximately $400,000, but his portfolio value has grown to over $2 million due to leverage and appreciation. This example illustrates the power of scaling through leverage and refinancing. By recycling capital and maintaining strong property performance, Ryan is able to build a portfolio that generates substantial income.

It also highlights the importance of discipline and strategy. Each property must meet specific criteria, and each step must be executed carefully. Scaling is not about speed—it is about consistency and alignment.

As you apply these principles to your own investing journey, consider how your first property can serve as the foundation for a larger system. With the right approach, you can transform a single investment into a portfolio that creates long-term financial freedom.

Chapter 8

Refinancing, Cash-Out Strategies, and Equity Recycling for Airbnb Investors

Once you have acquired and stabilized your Airbnb property, the next phase of growth is not just about holding the asset—it is about unlocking its full financial potential. One of the most powerful advantages of real estate investing is the ability to access equity without selling the property. This is where refinancing, cash-out strategies, and equity recycling come into play. These tools allow you to turn one successful investment into multiple income-producing assets, accelerating your path to building a scalable portfolio.

Refinancing is the process of replacing your existing loan with a new one, typically with different terms. For Airbnb investors, refinancing can serve multiple purposes. It can reduce your interest rate, improve your cash flow, extend your loan term, or most importantly, allow you to extract equity from the property. Understanding when and how to refinance is a critical skill that separates passive investors from strategic portfolio builders.

The most common type of refinance used in Airbnb investing is the cash-out refinance. In this scenario, you refinance your property at a higher loan amount than your current balance and receive the difference in cash. This cash can then be used for down payments, renovations, reserves, or acquiring additional properties. The ability to pull out capital without selling the asset is what makes real estate such a powerful wealth-building tool.

However, lenders do not allow unlimited access to equity. Most DSCR and Non-QM lenders will cap the loan-to-value ratio (LTV) for a cash-out refinance, typically between 70% and 75% for investment properties. This means that you must have sufficient equity in the property to make the refinance worthwhile. Equity can be created through appreciation, forced value (such as renovations), or a combination of both.

Timing is another critical factor in refinancing. Many lenders require a seasoning period, often six to twelve months, before allowing a cash-out refinance. This period ensures that the property has stabilized and that income projections are supported by actual performance. During this time, your focus should be on optimizing the property's income, improving guest experience, and building a strong track record.

Income performance plays a significant role in refinance approval. Just as with initial acquisition, lenders evaluate the property's DSCR. If your property's income has increased due to better management or market conditions, this can improve your DSCR and allow you to qualify for a larger loan amount. This is why operational excellence is not just about cash flow—it directly impacts your ability to scale.

Another important concept is equity recycling. This strategy involves continuously pulling equity from one property and reinvesting it into new properties. Instead of saving for each new down payment, you use the value created in your existing portfolio to fund future acquisitions. This creates a cycle of growth where each property contributes to the expansion of your portfolio.

For example, you may purchase a property, improve its performance, refinance to extract equity, and then use that equity to acquire another property. By repeating this process, you can grow your portfolio more rapidly than relying solely on personal savings. This is the foundation of scalable real estate investing.

It is also important to consider the impact of refinancing on your cash flow. While a cash-out refinance provides immediate capital, it also increases your loan balance and monthly payment. This can reduce your cash flow if not managed carefully. The key is to ensure that the property's income can support the new loan terms while still providing a margin of safety. Interest rates play a significant role in refinancing decisions. Refinancing at a higher interest rate may reduce your immediate cash flow, but if the extracted equity allows you to acquire additional high-performing properties, the overall portfolio may benefit. This requires a strategic approach, balancing short-term cash flow with long-term growth.

Another refinancing strategy involves rate-and-term refinancing, where the goal is to improve loan terms rather than extract equity. This may be useful if interest rates decrease or if you want to transition from a short-term or adjustable-rate loan to a long-term fixed-rate structure. Stability in financing can be an important component of long-term sustainability.

Bridge loans and short-term financing can also play a role in equity recycling. These loans allow investors to acquire properties quickly, improve them, and then refinance into long-term DSCR loans. While these strategies involve higher risk and cost, they can be highly effective when executed correctly.

As your portfolio grows, you may also explore portfolio-level refinancing. Instead of refinancing individual properties, you may be able to refinance multiple properties under a single loan. This can simplify management and potentially provide better terms, depending on the lender and your overall portfolio performance. Tax considerations are another important aspect of refinancing. Cash-out refinance proceeds are generally not considered taxable income because they are treated as loan proceeds rather than earnings. This allows investors to access capital without triggering immediate tax liabilities. However, it is important to consult with a tax professional to understand the implications for your specific situation.

Risk management is critical when using refinancing and equity recycling strategies. Over-leveraging can create vulnerability, especially during market downturns or periods of reduced income. Maintaining strong DSCR ratios, adequate reserves, and conservative assumptions helps mitigate this risk. The goal is to grow your portfolio sustainably, not to maximize leverage at the expense of stability.

Another key factor is property selection. Not all properties are equally suited for refinancing and equity extraction. Properties in strong markets with high demand and appreciation potential are more likely to generate the equity needed for successful refinancing. Additionally, properties with strong income performance are more likely to meet DSCR requirements for larger loan amounts.

Your long-term strategy should guide your refinancing decisions. Are you focused on rapid growth, or are you prioritizing stable cash flow? Are you building a portfolio for income, appreciation, or both? Understanding your objectives helps you determine when to refinance, how much equity to extract, and how to allocate that capital.

Ultimately, refinancing and equity recycling are about maximizing the efficiency of your capital. Instead of letting equity sit idle, you put it to work, generating additional income and expanding your portfolio. This approach transforms real estate from a static investment into a dynamic system that grows over time.

The key takeaway from this chapter is that refinancing is not just a financial transaction–it is a strategic tool. When used correctly, it allows you to unlock value, accelerate growth, and build a scalable Airbnb portfolio. By understanding the mechanics, timing, and risks involved, you can use these strategies to move beyond single-property ownership and into long-term wealth creation.

Using Cash-Out Refinance to Acquire Multiple Airbnb Properties

Let's walk through a detailed example of how an investor named Daniel uses refinancing and equity recycling to grow his Airbnb portfolio.

Daniel purchases his first Airbnb property for $400,000 with a 25% down payment of $100,000. His initial loan amount is $300,000 at a 7.75% interest rate, resulting in a monthly housing expense of $2,800. The property generates net operating income of $4,200, giving him a DSCR of 1.50 and monthly cash flow of $1,400.

After one year, Daniel improves the property's performance through better management and upgrades. At the same time, the market appreciates, increasing the property's value to $460,000.

Daniel decides to perform a cash-out refinance at 75% LTV. This allows him to obtain a new loan of $345,000. After paying off the original loan balance of $295,000, he receives approximately $50,000 in cash.

His new loan has a slightly higher monthly payment of $3,000 due to the increased loan amount. However, the property's improved income now generates $4,500 in net operating income, resulting in a DSCR of 1.50 and maintaining strong cash flow.

Daniel uses the $50,000 from the refinance as a down payment for a second property priced at $200,000. He secures a DSCR loan for this property with a 25% down payment and begins generating an additional $1,000 per month in cash flow.

Now, Daniel has two properties generating a combined monthly cash flow of $2,400. After another year, both properties appreciate and perform well. Daniel repeats the refinancing process on his second property, extracting $30,000 in equity. He combines this with savings to purchase a third property.

By the time Daniel owns three properties, his total monthly cash flow reaches approximately $3,800. He continues this process, carefully managing risk and ensuring each property meets DSCR requirements.

After five years, Daniel owns five Airbnb properties with a combined value of $2.2 million. His total monthly cash flow exceeds $7,000, and his portfolio continues to grow through appreciation and income optimization.

This example demonstrates how refinancing and equity recycling can transform a single investment into a multi-property portfolio. It highlights the importance of timing, performance, and strategic planning.

It also shows that growth is not dependent on large amounts of initial capital, but on the efficient use of available resources. By leveraging equity and reinvesting it wisely, investors can accelerate their progress and build substantial wealth over time.

As you consider your own strategy, think about how each property can serve as a stepping stone to the next. With the right approach, refinancing becomes more than a tool—it becomes the engine that drives your entire investment portfolio forward.

Chapter 9

Financing Multi-Unit Airbnb Properties (2–4 Units and Small Multifamily)

As you advance in your Airbnb investing journey, one of the most powerful ways to accelerate growth is by moving into multi-unit properties. Duplexes, triplexes, fourplexes, and small multifamily buildings offer a unique opportunity to generate multiple income streams from a single asset. In the context of Airbnb financing, these properties introduce both advantages and complexities that require a deeper understanding of underwriting, income modeling, and deal structuring.

Multi-unit Airbnb properties differ from single-family investments in one critical way: they allow you to diversify income within a single property. Instead of relying on one unit to generate revenue, you have multiple units contributing to total income. This can significantly improve stability and reduce risk. If one unit experiences lower occupancy, the other units can help offset the loss. From a lender's perspective, this diversification can strengthen the overall loan profile—provided the numbers are structured correctly. However, financing multi-unit properties for Airbnb use is not as straightforward as financing single-family homes. Lenders must consider how each unit will be used, whether the property complies with zoning regulations, and how income will be calculated. Some lenders may treat a 2–4 unit property as residential, while others may evaluate it more like a commercial asset, especially if all units are used for short-term rentals.

One of the first distinctions to understand is how income is calculated across multiple units. Instead of analyzing a single income stream, lenders evaluate the combined income of all units. This includes the average daily rate and occupancy for each unit, as well as the overall performance of the property. In some cases, lenders may apply conservative assumptions to account for variability across units.

For example, a duplex with two Airbnb units may generate income from both units simultaneously. If each unit has an average daily rate of $180 and an occupancy rate of 70%, the combined income can be significantly higher than a single-family property. However, expenses also increase, as each unit requires cleaning, utilities, maintenance, and management. Understanding how to balance these factors is essential for achieving a strong DSCR.

Another important consideration is zoning and compliance. Multi-unit properties are often subject to stricter regulations than single-family homes. Some municipalities allow short-term rentals in single-family properties but restrict them in multi-unit buildings. Others may require specific licenses or impose limits on the number of units that can be used for Airbnb. Before purchasing a multi-unit property, it is critical to verify that your intended use is permitted.

Lenders are increasingly aware of these regulatory factors and may require documentation confirming compliance. In some cases, they may limit financing for properties in areas with uncertain or restrictive regulations. As an investor, choosing properties in Airbnb-friendly markets can simplify the approval process and reduce risk.

Financing options for multi-unit Airbnb properties typically include DSCR loans and Non-QM loans. Traditional loans may also be available for 2–4 unit properties, particularly if one unit is owner-occupied. However, traditional loans often rely on long-term rental income, which may undervalue the property's true earning potential as a short-term rental.

DSCR loans are often the preferred option for multi-unit Airbnb investments because they focus on property income rather than personal income. Lenders evaluate the combined net operating income of all units and compare it to the total housing expense. As long as the DSCR meets the required threshold, the loan can be approved. One advantage of multi-unit properties is the potential for higher DSCR ratios. Because income is generated from multiple units, the total revenue can significantly exceed the mortgage payment, especially in strong markets. This can make it easier to qualify and provide a larger margin of safety.

However, multi-unit properties also require more capital. Purchase prices are typically higher, and down payment requirements may be more substantial. In addition, operating costs are higher due to the increased number of units. Investors must be prepared to manage these costs and maintain sufficient reserves.

Another important factor is property management. Managing multiple units within a single property can be more complex than managing a single-family home. This includes coordinating bookings, cleaning schedules, maintenance, and guest communication across multiple units. Many investors choose to hire professional management companies to handle these responsibilities, which can improve consistency but also increase expenses.

Hybrid strategies are also possible with multi-unit properties. For example, an investor may choose to operate some units as short-term rentals while renting others on a long-term basis.

This can provide a balance between stable income and higher short-term rental returns. Lenders may consider both income streams when evaluating the property, depending on the loan program.

Another strategy involves house hacking, where the investor lives in one unit and rents out the others as Airbnb properties. This can allow access to traditional financing with lower down payment requirements while still generating significant income. However, this approach must comply with local regulations and lender guidelines.

Scaling with multi-unit properties can be highly efficient. Instead of acquiring multiple single-family homes, an investor can acquire one property with multiple income streams. This reduces transaction costs, simplifies financing, and allows for centralized management. It also accelerates portfolio growth by increasing income per acquisition.

Risk management remains critical in multi-unit investing. While income diversification reduces risk, it does not eliminate it. Market fluctuations, regulatory changes, and operational challenges can still impact performance. Maintaining strong DSCR ratios, reserves, and management systems is essential for long-term success.

Another important concept is valuation. Multi-unit properties may be valued based on income rather than comparable sales, especially if they are treated as commercial assets. This can create opportunities for investors to increase value through improved performance. By optimizing income, you can potentially increase the property's value and create additional equity.

Ultimately, financing multi-unit Airbnb properties requires a combination of strategic planning, market knowledge, and financial discipline. The potential rewards are significant, but so are the complexities. By understanding how lenders evaluate these properties and how to structure deals effectively, you can unlock a powerful pathway to scaling your Airbnb portfolio.

Analyzing a Duplex Airbnb Investment for DSCR and Profitability

Let's analyze a real-life example of an investor named Kevin who is evaluating a duplex Airbnb property priced at $600,000.

Kevin plans to put 25% down, which equals $150,000, resulting in a loan amount of $450,000. He secures a DSCR loan at a 7.75% interest rate, with a monthly principal and interest payment of approximately $3,222. Including taxes, insurance, and other expenses, his total monthly housing cost is $4,200.

The duplex consists of two identical units. Kevin researches comparable Airbnb data and finds that each unit has an average daily rate of $190 and an occupancy rate of 70%. To calculate gross monthly revenue, Kevin multiplies the ADR by the number of days in a month and adjusts for occupancy. For each unit, this results in $3,990 in monthly revenue. For both units combined, the total gross monthly revenue is $7,980.

Next, Kevin estimates operating expenses at 30% of gross revenue, reflecting the higher costs associated with managing multiple units. This equals $2,394. Subtracting this from the gross revenue results in a net operating income of $5,586.

To calculate the DSCR, Kevin divides the net operating income by the total housing expense. In this case, $5,586 divided by $4,200 results in a DSCR of 1.33, which exceeds the lender's requirement.

Kevin then analyzes cash flow. With net operating income of $5,586 and housing expenses of $4,200, his monthly cash flow is $1,386, or $16,632 annually.

To improve performance, Kevin considers adding amenities such as upgraded furnishings, smart home features, and enhanced outdoor space. These improvements increase the average daily rate to $210 and occupancy to 75%.

With these adjustments, each unit generates $4,725 in monthly revenue, resulting in total gross revenue of $9,450. After expenses, the net operating income increases to $6,615. With the same housing expense of $4,200, the DSCR rises to 1.58, and monthly cash flow increases to $2,415.

This example demonstrates the power of multi-unit Airbnb investing. By combining multiple income streams within a single property, Kevin is able to achieve strong DSCR, significant cash flow, and improved scalability.

It also highlights the importance of optimization. Small improvements in pricing and occupancy can have a large impact when applied across multiple units. This creates opportunities for investors to increase both income and property value.

As you consider multi-unit investments, think about how these principles apply to your strategy. With the right approach, multi-unit Airbnb properties can become a cornerstone of your portfolio, providing both stability and growth.

Chapter 10

Advanced Airbnb Mortgage Loan Structuring Using DSCR, Asset-Based, and Creative Financing

As you reach this stage in your Airbnb investing journey, you are no longer thinking like a beginner—you are thinking like a strategist. You understand how to qualify for loans, analyze income, and structure deals for approval. Now, the next level is mastering advanced loan structuring. This is where elite investors separate themselves from the average. They do not rely on one financing method—they combine multiple strategies to close deals that others cannot, scale faster, and optimize both cash flow and long-term equity growth.

Advanced Airbnb mortgage structuring is about flexibility. Every deal is different, and the ability to adapt your financing approach to fit the deal is a powerful advantage. Instead of asking, "What loan can I get?" you begin asking, "How can I structure this deal using multiple financing tools to make it work?" This shift in thinking opens up opportunities that are invisible to most investors.

The foundation of advanced structuring begins with DSCR loans. As you already know, DSCR loans allow you to qualify based on property income rather than personal income. However, at an advanced level, DSCR loans are not just used individually—they are layered strategically. For example, you might use a DSCR loan for acquisition, then refinance into another DSCR loan after increasing income, or combine DSCR with other financing sources to reduce capital requirements.

One powerful strategy involves pairing DSCR loans with asset-based lending. Asset-based loans allow borrowers to qualify using liquid assets such as bank accounts, brokerage accounts, or retirement funds. Instead of relying on income, lenders calculate your ability to repay based on your asset base. This is particularly useful for high-net-worth investors or those with significant liquidity but limited reportable income.

By combining DSCR and asset-based strategies, you can create a hybrid structure where the property qualifies based on income while your assets provide additional support. This can lead to higher approval amounts, better terms, or the ability to close deals that might otherwise fall short of DSCR requirements.

Another advanced technique is using cross-collateralization. This involves leveraging equity from one property to secure financing for another. Instead of relying solely on cash for a down payment, you use the value of your existing assets. This allows you to preserve liquidity while continuing to expand your portfolio. However, this strategy must be used carefully, as it ties multiple properties together and increases overall risk.

Creative financing is another powerful tool in advanced structuring. This includes seller financing, subject-to transactions, and partnerships. Seller financing allows you to negotiate terms directly with the seller, potentially reducing or eliminating the need for traditional lending. Subject-to deals involve taking over an existing mortgage while acquiring the property. These strategies can be particularly useful in situations where traditional financing is not ideal.

Partnerships also play a significant role in advanced structuring. By partnering with other investors, you can combine capital, credit, and expertise to complete larger deals. For example, one partner may provide the down payment, while another manages the property. This allows you to scale beyond the limitations of your individual resources.

Another advanced approach is layering financing within a single deal. For example, you might use a DSCR loan for 75% of the purchase price, a HELOC or second mortgage for part of the down payment, and your own capital for the remainder. This reduces your out-of-pocket investment while maintaining control of the property. However, it also increases leverage, so careful analysis is required. Interest-only loans are another tool used in advanced structuring. These loans allow you to pay only the interest for a specified period, reducing your monthly payments and increasing cash flow. While this can improve short-term performance, it does not reduce the principal balance, so it must be used strategically.

Bridge loans are often used for transitional properties that require improvements. These short-term loans allow you to acquire and renovate a property quickly, then refinance into a long-term DSCR loan once the property is stabilized. This approach is particularly effective for properties with untapped income potential.

Another key concept is optimizing loan terms rather than just focusing on approval. This includes negotiating interest rates, prepayment penalties, and loan duration. For example, a slightly higher interest rate with no prepayment penalty may provide more flexibility for refinancing in the future. Understanding these trade-offs allows you to structure loans that align with your long-term strategy.

Advanced investors also focus on portfolio-level optimization. Instead of evaluating each property in isolation, they consider how each loan fits within the overall portfolio. This includes balancing risk, maintaining strong DSCR ratios, and ensuring that cash flow remains positive across all properties. Risk management becomes even more important at this level. As leverage increases, so does exposure to market fluctuations. Maintaining reserves, diversifying markets, and avoiding over-leveraging are essential for long-term sustainability. Advanced structuring is not about taking excessive risk—it is about using leverage intelligently.

Another important aspect is timing. Knowing when to refinance, when to hold, and when to sell is critical. Market conditions, interest rates, and property performance all influence these decisions. Advanced investors continuously monitor these factors and adjust their strategy accordingly.

Tax efficiency is also a key consideration. Structuring deals through entities, leveraging depreciation, and using refinancing strategically can significantly impact your after-tax returns. Working with experienced professionals can help you optimize your structure and maximize benefits.

Ultimately, advanced Airbnb mortgage structuring is about control. It allows you to control more assets with less capital, adapt to changing conditions, and create a system that supports long-term growth. It is the bridge between being an investor and becoming a real estate entrepreneur.

The key takeaway from this chapter is that there are always multiple ways to structure a deal. By understanding and combining different financing strategies, you can unlock opportunities, overcome obstacles, and build a portfolio that continues to grow over time.

Structuring an Advanced Airbnb Deal Using Multiple Financing Strategies

Let's analyze a scenario where an investor named Michael structures a complex Airbnb deal using multiple financing methods.

Michael identifies a property priced at $800,000 in a high-demand Airbnb market. The property has strong income potential but requires strategic financing to make the deal work.

Instead of using a traditional 25% down payment ($200,000), Michael structures the deal using a combination of financing sources.

First, he secures a DSCR loan for 75% of the purchase price, which equals $600,000. At a 7.75% interest rate, his monthly principal and interest payment is approximately $4,300. Including taxes and insurance, his total monthly housing expense is $5,200.

Next, Michael uses a HELOC from another property to cover $100,000 of the down payment. He contributes $100,000 of his own capital, reducing his out-of-pocket investment.

The property generates an average daily rate of $320 with an occupancy rate of 72%. This results in gross monthly revenue of $6,912. After deducting 25% for expenses ($1,728), the net operating income is $5,184.

At this stage, the DSCR is slightly below 1.0, meaning the deal does not initially qualify. However, Michael implements an improvement strategy.

He invests $50,000 in upgrades, including luxury furnishings, a pool, and enhanced outdoor space. These improvements increase the average daily rate to $380 and occupancy to 75%.

With these changes, the gross monthly revenue increases to $8,550. After expenses, the net operating income rises to $6,412.

Now, dividing the net operating income by the housing expense of $5,200 results in a DSCR of 1.23, allowing the loan to qualify.

Michael also analyzes cash flow. With net operating income of $6,412 and housing expenses of $5,200, his monthly cash flow is $1,212, or $14,544 annually.

Next, Michael plans for refinancing. After one year of strong performance, the property value increases to $920,000. He refinances at 75% LTV, resulting in a new loan of $690,000. After paying off the original loan, he extracts approximately $90,000 in equity, which he uses to fund his next acquisition.

This example demonstrates how advanced structuring can transform a challenging deal into a successful investment. By combining DSCR financing, HELOC funds, property improvements, and refinancing, Michael is able to acquire, optimize, and scale.

It also highlights the importance of strategy. Each step—from acquisition to improvement to refinancing—is carefully planned to maximize both approval and profitability.

As you move forward, consider how these advanced techniques can be applied to your own deals. With the right approach, you can structure transactions that not only work—but create momentum for long-term growth and financial freedom.

Chapter 11

Building Systems, Automation, and Operations for a Scalable Airbnb Business

As your Airbnb portfolio grows, the challenge shifts from acquiring properties to managing them efficiently. Many investors underestimate this transition. Owning one Airbnb property can feel manageable, but owning multiple properties quickly becomes complex without systems in place. This is where operations, automation, and scalable systems become the foundation of long-term success.

In the early stages, you may be able to handle bookings, guest communication, cleaning coordination, and pricing adjustments manually. However, as your portfolio expands, this approach becomes unsustainable. The key to scaling is not working harder—it is building systems that allow your business to operate efficiently with minimal friction.

The first step in building a scalable Airbnb operation is standardization. Every property should follow a consistent framework, from listing setup to guest communication to cleaning procedures. Standardization reduces errors, improves efficiency, and creates a predictable experience for guests. This consistency also makes it easier to train team members or outsource tasks as your business grows.

Listing optimization is one of the most important components of your system. Each property should have professional photography, compelling descriptions, and a clear value proposition. High-quality listings attract more bookings, improve occupancy, and allow you to command higher rates. As you scale, having a repeatable process for creating and optimizing listings ensures that every property performs at a high level from the start.

Pricing strategy is another critical area where systems and automation can make a significant impact. Airbnb pricing is dynamic, influenced by demand, seasonality, local events, and competition. Manual pricing adjustments can be time-consuming and inconsistent. Many investors use dynamic pricing tools that automatically adjust rates based on market conditions. These tools help maximize revenue while maintaining competitive positioning.

Guest communication is a core part of the Airbnb experience. Prompt, professional communication leads to better reviews and higher occupancy. However, managing messages across multiple properties can quickly become overwhelming. Automation tools allow you to create templates for common interactions, such as booking confirmations, check-in instructions, and follow-up messages. This ensures consistent communication while reducing the time required to manage inquiries.

Cleaning and maintenance are operational pillars that directly impact guest satisfaction. A clean, well-maintained property is essential for positive reviews and repeat bookings. As your portfolio grows, coordinating cleaning schedules becomes more complex. Many investors use scheduling software or work with cleaning companies that specialize in short-term rentals. Establishing clear standards and checklists ensures that every property meets your quality expectations.

Maintenance systems are equally important. Properties require ongoing upkeep, from minor repairs to major improvements. Having a network of reliable contractors and a process for handling maintenance requests ensures that issues are resolved quickly. This minimizes disruptions to guests and protects your investment.

Another key component of scalable operations is channel management. Many investors list their properties on multiple platforms, such as Airbnb, VRBO, and Booking.com. Managing availability, pricing, and bookings across these platforms manually can lead to errors and double bookings.

Channel management software synchronizes listings across platforms, ensuring accuracy and maximizing exposure.

Financial tracking is an often-overlooked aspect of Airbnb operations. As your portfolio grows, it becomes essential to track income, expenses, and performance metrics for each property. This includes monitoring occupancy rates, average daily rates, net operating income, and cash flow. Financial software or spreadsheets can help you analyze performance and make data-driven decisions.

Automation also extends to financial management. Tools that integrate with booking platforms can automatically track revenue, categorize expenses, and generate reports. This reduces administrative work and provides real-time insights into your business.

Team building is another critical factor in scaling operations. While automation can handle many tasks, human support is still necessary for certain aspects of the business. This may include property managers, cleaning staff, maintenance personnel, and customer support. Building a reliable team allows you to delegate responsibilities and focus on growth and strategy.

One of the most important decisions you will make is whether to self-manage or hire professional management.

Self-management offers greater control and higher profit margins but requires more time and effort. Professional management provides convenience and scalability but comes at a cost. Many investors start by self-managing and transition to professional management as their portfolio grows.

Technology plays a central role in modern Airbnb operations. From smart locks and automated check-in systems to noise monitoring devices and energy management tools, technology enhances efficiency and guest experience. These tools reduce manual work, improve security, and provide valuable data for decision-making.

Another important concept is creating a seamless guest experience. From the moment a guest books your property to the time they check out, every interaction should be smooth and professional. This includes clear instructions, responsive communication, and a well-prepared property. A positive guest experience leads to higher ratings, better reviews, and increased bookings.

As your business grows, it is important to continuously refine your systems. What works for one property may need adjustment for multiple properties. Regularly reviewing your processes, identifying inefficiencies, and implementing improvements ensures that your operations remain effective.

Scalability also requires resilience. Systems should be designed to handle unexpected challenges, such as last-minute cancellations, maintenance issues, or changes in demand. Having contingency plans and backup resources ensures that your business can adapt to disruptions.

Another key aspect of scaling is time management. As an investor, your time should be focused on high-value activities, such as acquiring new properties, analyzing deals, and optimizing your portfolio. By delegating operational tasks and leveraging automation, you can free up time to focus on growth.

Branding is another consideration as you scale. Creating a recognizable brand for your Airbnb properties can differentiate you from competitors and attract repeat guests. This may include consistent design elements, branding across listings, and a focus on delivering a unique experience.

Ultimately, building systems and automation is about creating a business that runs efficiently without constant oversight. It allows you to scale your portfolio, improve performance, and achieve long-term sustainability. Without these systems, growth becomes chaotic and difficult to manage.

The key takeaway from this chapter is that success in Airbnb investing is not just about acquiring properties—it is about building a system that supports those properties. By implementing strong operations, leveraging technology, and creating scalable processes, you can transform your portfolio into a well-functioning business.

Scaling Operations and Increasing Profit Through Automation

Let's examine an investor named Lisa who owns three Airbnb properties and wants to scale to six while improving efficiency and profitability.

Each of Lisa's three properties generates the following monthly performance:

- Gross monthly revenue: $5,500 per property
- Operating expenses (manual management): 30% ($1,650)
- Net operating income per property: $3,850
- Monthly mortgage and fixed costs: $2,800
- Monthly cash flow per property: $1,050

With three properties, Lisa's total monthly cash flow is $3,150.

However, Lisa spends approximately 25 hours per week managing bookings, communication, cleaning coordination, and pricing adjustments. This limits her ability to acquire new properties and scale her business.

Lisa decides to implement automation and systems.

First, she adopts dynamic pricing software, which increases her average daily rate and occupancy slightly. This raises her gross monthly revenue from $5,500 to $5,900 per property.

Next, she implements automated messaging, reducing the time spent on guest communication. She also partners with a cleaning company that offers discounted rates due to volume, reducing her cleaning costs.

Her operating expenses decrease from 30% to 27%, or $1,593 per property.

Her new net operating income per property becomes $4,307.

With the same mortgage cost of $2,800, her monthly cash flow increases to $1,507 per property.

Across three properties, her total monthly cash flow increases to $4,521, an increase of $1,371 per month.

More importantly, her time commitment decreases from 25 hours per week to 10 hours per week. With the additional time and improved cash flow, Lisa acquires three more properties with similar performance. Now with six properties, each generating $1,507 per month, her total monthly cash flow reaches $9,042, or over $108,000 annually.

Her total time commitment increases slightly to 18 hours per week due to scaling, but remains manageable due to automation and systems.

This example demonstrates the power of operations and automation. By improving efficiency, Lisa not only increases profitability but also frees up time to scale her portfolio.

It highlights that scaling is not just about acquiring more properties—it is about improving the performance and efficiency of each property.

As you build your Airbnb business, consider how systems and automation can enhance your operations. With the right approach, you can create a portfolio that generates significant income while remaining manageable and sustainable.

Chapter 12

Exit Strategies, Portfolio Optimization, and Long-Term Wealth Creation with Airbnb Investments

As you reach this stage in your Airbnb investing journey, you have learned how to acquire properties, qualify for financing, optimize income, and scale your portfolio. However, one of the most important aspects of real estate investing is often overlooked: the exit strategy. Knowing how and when to exit—or reposition—your investments is just as important as knowing how to acquire them. In this final chapter, you will learn how to optimize your portfolio, plan strategic exits, and build long-term wealth through Airbnb investments.

An exit strategy is not simply about selling a property. It is about having a clear plan for how each asset fits into your overall financial goals. This includes decisions about holding, refinancing, converting, or selling properties based on market conditions, performance, and personal objectives. A well-defined exit strategy provides flexibility and ensures that you can adapt to changes in the market.

One of the most common exit strategies in Airbnb investing is the long-term hold. In this approach, you retain ownership of the property and continue to generate income over time. This strategy benefits from both cash flow and appreciation. As property values increase and loan balances decrease, your equity grows, creating long-term wealth. For many investors, this is the foundation of financial independence.

However, holding a property indefinitely is not always the optimal strategy. Market conditions can change, regulations can evolve, and property performance can fluctuate. In some cases, selling a property may provide a better return than continuing to hold it. Understanding when to sell—and how to maximize value—is a critical skill.

Another common strategy is refinancing and holding. Instead of selling, you refinance the property to access equity while retaining ownership. This allows you to continue generating income while using the extracted capital to invest in additional properties. This approach aligns with the concept of equity recycling discussed in earlier chapters and is a key driver of portfolio growth.

Portfolio optimization involves continuously evaluating your properties to ensure they are performing at their highest potential. This includes analyzing metrics such as cash flow, DSCR, occupancy rates, and return on investment. Properties that underperform may need to be improved, repositioned, or replaced. Optimization is an ongoing process that ensures your portfolio remains efficient and profitable.

Another important exit strategy is conversion. In some cases, it may be advantageous to convert an Airbnb property into a long-term rental or vice versa. This flexibility allows you to adapt to changing market conditions. For example, if short-term rental regulations become restrictive, converting to a long-term rental can preserve income. Conversely, if market demand for short-term rentals increases, converting a long-term rental can boost profitability.

The 1031 exchange is a powerful tool for investors looking to defer taxes when selling a property. This strategy allows you to reinvest the proceeds from a sale into another property without immediately paying capital gains taxes. By using a 1031 exchange, you can upgrade to larger or more profitable properties while preserving your capital. This is a key strategy for long-term wealth accumulation.

Timing plays a critical role in exit strategies. Selling during a strong market can maximize your return, while holding during a downturn may allow you to benefit from future appreciation. Understanding market cycles and trends helps you make informed decisions about when to exit or reposition your investments. Another important consideration is debt management. As your portfolio grows, managing debt becomes increasingly important. Refinancing, paying down loans, or restructuring debt can improve cash flow and reduce risk. Balancing leverage with stability is essential for long-term success.

Cash flow remains a central focus in portfolio optimization. Properties that generate strong, consistent cash flow provide stability and flexibility. They allow you to reinvest in new opportunities, cover expenses, and build reserves. Prioritizing cash flow ensures that your portfolio can sustain itself over time.

Appreciation is another key component of wealth creation. While cash flow provides immediate income, appreciation increases your net worth over time. Properties in strong markets with high demand are more likely to appreciate, creating opportunities for refinancing or selling at a profit.

Diversification is an important strategy for reducing risk and enhancing stability. By investing in different markets, property types, and price points, you can protect your portfolio from localized downturns. Diversification also allows you to take advantage of different opportunities across markets.

Another critical aspect of long-term wealth creation is tax strategy. Real estate offers numerous tax advantages, including depreciation, deductions, and deferral strategies. Understanding how to leverage these benefits can significantly improve your overall returns. Working with a knowledgeable tax professional ensures that you maximize these opportunities.

Estate planning is also an important consideration for long-term investors. Real estate can be a powerful tool for building generational wealth. Structuring your portfolio in a way that allows for efficient transfer of assets ensures that your investments benefit future generations.

As your portfolio matures, your focus may shift from growth to preservation. This involves reducing risk, stabilizing income, and protecting your assets. Strategies such as paying down debt, diversifying investments, and maintaining reserves become increasingly important.

Another advanced concept is portfolio-level analysis. Instead of evaluating properties individually, you analyze the performance of your entire portfolio. This includes overall cash flow, average DSCR, total equity, and return on investment. This holistic view allows you to make strategic decisions that enhance the performance of your entire portfolio.

Liquidity is another important factor in exit planning. Real estate is not a liquid asset, meaning it cannot be easily converted to cash. Maintaining access to liquidity through reserves, lines of credit, or refinancing ensures that you can respond to opportunities and challenges.

Ultimately, the goal of Airbnb investing is not just to acquire properties, but to build a system that generates long-term wealth. This requires a combination of strategic planning, disciplined execution, and continuous optimization. By understanding exit strategies and portfolio management, you can ensure that your investments align with your financial goals.

The key takeaway from this chapter is that success in Airbnb investing is not defined by the number of properties you own, but by how effectively those properties work together to create income, equity, and long-term value. With the right strategies, you can transform your portfolio into a powerful engine for wealth creation.

Optimizing a Portfolio and Executing an Exit Strategy

Let's analyze a scenario where an investor named David owns a portfolio of four Airbnb properties and is evaluating his exit and optimization strategy.

Each property has the following characteristics:

- Property value: $500,000
- Loan balance: $350,000
- Monthly net operating income: $4,500
- Monthly housing expense: $3,200
- Monthly cash flow per property: $1,300

With four properties, David's total monthly cash flow is $5,200, or $62,400 annually.

Over time, the market appreciates, and each property's value increases to $600,000. David now has $250,000 in equity per property, or $1,000,000 in total equity across his portfolio.

David evaluates three options: hold, refinance, or sell.

If he chooses to hold, he continues generating $62,400 annually while benefiting from further appreciation.

If he chooses to refinance at 75% LTV, he can access $450,000 per property. After paying off the existing loan, he can extract $100,000 per property, or $400,000 total. This capital can be used to acquire additional properties.

However, refinancing increases his loan balance and monthly payments. His new monthly housing expense rises to $3,800 per property. With the same net operating income of $4,500, his cash flow decreases to $700 per property. With four properties, his total monthly cash flow becomes $2,800, or $33,600 annually, but he now has $400,000 in capital to reinvest.

If David uses this $400,000 to acquire two additional properties, each generating $1,200 in monthly cash flow, his total portfolio expands to six properties.

His new total monthly cash flow becomes:

- Existing properties: $2,800
- New properties: $2,400
- Total: $5,200 per month

Despite reduced cash flow per property, his overall income remains stable while his portfolio grows.

Alternatively, David considers selling one property. By selling at $600,000 and paying off the loan, he nets approximately $250,000. After transaction costs, he retains $230,000.

He can use this capital to acquire a larger multi-unit property generating $2,500 in monthly cash flow, replacing the $1,300 from the sold property.

This increases his overall portfolio cash flow while consolidating assets. This example illustrates how different exit strategies impact both cash flow and growth. Holding provides stability, refinancing enables expansion, and selling allows for repositioning.

It demonstrates that there is no single “best” strategy. The optimal choice depends on your goals, market conditions, and risk tolerance.

As you apply these concepts, consider how each decision affects your long-term objectives. By aligning your exit strategy with your financial goals, you can create a portfolio that not only grows but also supports your vision for the future.

Chapter 13

Creating a Repeatable Deal-Finding and Financing System for Airbnb Investments

At this stage in your journey, you understand how Airbnb financing works, how to structure deals, how to scale, and how to manage a portfolio. The final evolution is turning everything you've learned into a repeatable system—a machine that consistently finds, analyzes, finances, and closes profitable Airbnb deals. This is where investing transitions from occasional success to predictable results.

Most investors struggle not because they lack knowledge, but because they lack systems. They rely on random opportunities, inconsistent analysis, and reactive decision-making. A repeatable system removes guesswork. It allows you to identify high-quality deals quickly, evaluate them accurately, and move forward with confidence. This system becomes your competitive advantage.

The foundation of your system begins with deal sourcing. You need a consistent pipeline of potential properties. This includes using platforms such as MLS listings, off-market opportunities, wholesaler networks, direct marketing, and data-driven tools. The goal is not to find one deal—it is to create a flow of deals. When you have consistent opportunities, you can be selective and focus only on the best investments.

Market selection is a critical component of deal sourcing. Not all markets are equally suitable for Airbnb investments. Your system should include criteria for evaluating markets, such as tourism demand, occupancy trends, average daily rates, local regulations, and competition. By focusing on markets that meet your criteria, you increase the likelihood of finding profitable deals.

Once you identify potential properties, the next step is deal analysis. This is where your system must be precise and consistent. Every deal should be evaluated using the same framework, including purchase price, projected income, operating expenses, DSCR, cash flow, and return on investment. By standardizing your analysis, you can quickly compare opportunities and identify the best ones.

Speed is an important advantage in competitive markets. A well-defined system allows you to analyze deals quickly and make decisions without hesitation. This does not mean rushing—it means being prepared. When you know your criteria and trust your process, you can act decisively. Financing is the next layer of your system. Instead of searching for a lender after finding a deal, you should have financing options ready in advance. This includes relationships with DSCR lenders, Non-QM lenders, and other financing sources. Pre-qualification and understanding your borrowing capacity allow you to move quickly when opportunities arise.

Your system should also include deal structuring strategies. This means knowing how to adjust variables such as down payment, loan type, and income projections to meet lender requirements. When a deal does not initially qualify, your system should provide alternative approaches to make it work.

Another important component is due diligence. Before closing on a property, you must verify all assumptions. This includes confirming market data, reviewing property condition, understanding regulations, and validating income projections. A thorough due diligence process reduces risk and ensures that your deal aligns with your expectations.

Negotiation is another key skill within your system. The ability to negotiate purchase price, terms, and conditions can significantly impact your deal's performance. Successful investors understand that every dollar saved on acquisition improves both qualification and profitability.

Once a deal is under contract, your system should guide you through the closing process. This includes coordinating with lenders, appraisers, inspectors, and title companies. Having a clear process ensures that transactions move smoothly and efficiently.

After closing, your system transitions into stabilization and optimization. This involves setting up the property, launching the listing, and implementing your operational strategy. The goal is to achieve consistent performance as quickly as possible, which strengthens your position for future financing.

Tracking performance is another essential part of your system. By monitoring key metrics such as occupancy, average daily rate, and cash flow, you can identify opportunities for improvement. Data-driven decision-making allows you to continuously refine your approach and maximize results.

Automation plays a significant role in creating a repeatable system. Tools for pricing, communication, and management reduce manual work and improve efficiency. Automation ensures that your system can scale without becoming overwhelming.

Another important aspect is building a team. As your system grows, you will need support from real estate agents, lenders, contractors, cleaners, and property managers. A reliable team allows you to focus on high-level strategy while ensuring that operations run smoothly.

Consistency is the key to success. A repeatable system is only effective if it is used consistently. This means following your process for every deal, regardless of market conditions or external pressures. Discipline ensures that your results remain predictable.

Another critical concept is feedback and improvement. Your system should evolve over time based on experience and results. By analyzing past deals, identifying strengths and weaknesses, and making adjustments, you can continuously improve your system.

Scaling your system involves increasing the volume of deals while maintaining quality. This may include expanding into new markets, increasing your marketing efforts, or leveraging partnerships. The goal is to grow without compromising your standards.

Risk management is also integrated into your system. By maintaining reserves, diversifying your portfolio, and adhering to conservative assumptions, you can protect your investments and ensure long-term sustainability.

Your system should also align with your long-term goals. Whether you are focused on cash flow, appreciation, or portfolio growth, your system should support your objectives. This alignment ensures that every deal contributes to your overall strategy.

Ultimately, creating a repeatable deal-finding and financing system transforms your approach to Airbnb investing. It replaces uncertainty with structure, inconsistency with predictability, and effort with efficiency. This is the foundation of building a scalable, sustainable real estate business.

Building a Repeatable System That Produces Consistent Airbnb Deals

Let's examine an investor named Chris who builds a system to acquire two Airbnb properties per year.

Chris defines his criteria:

- Purchase price range: $300,000 to $500,000
- Minimum DSCR: 1.25
- Minimum monthly cash flow: $1,000
- Target occupancy: 65%–75%
- Target ADR: $200–$300

Chris reviews 50 properties per month using his system. Out of these, 10 meet his initial criteria. He performs detailed analysis on these 10 properties and identifies 3 strong deals. From these 3 deals, Chris successfully negotiates and closes on

1 property per month for two months, achieving his goal of 2 properties per year.

Let's analyze one of these deals.

Chris purchases a property for $400,000 with a 25% down payment of $100,000. His loan amount is $300,000, with a monthly housing expense of $2,800.

Using his system, he projects:

- ADR: $240
- Occupancy: 70%
- Gross monthly revenue: $5,040
- Operating expenses (25%): $1,260
- Net operating income: $3,780

His DSCR is 1.35, and his monthly cash flow is $980.

Chris then optimizes the property, increasing ADR to $260 and occupancy to 72%.

This raises:

- Gross monthly revenue to $5,616

- Net operating income to $4,212
- Monthly cash flow to $1,412
- DSCR to 1.50

Chris repeats this process for his second property, achieving similar results.

After one year, Chris owns two properties generating a combined monthly cash flow of approximately $2,800.

After three years, following the same system, Chris owns six properties generating over $8,000 per month in cash flow.

Because his system is consistent, his results are predictable. He knows how many deals to analyze, how many offers to make, and what performance to expect.

This example demonstrates the power of a repeatable system. It shows that success is not based on luck, but on process and discipline.

As you build your own system, focus on creating a framework that you can follow consistently. With the right system in place, you can turn Airbnb investing into a predictable and scalable business.

Chapter 14

Advanced Risk Management, Market Cycles, and Protecting Your Airbnb Portfolio

As your Airbnb portfolio grows and your financing strategies become more sophisticated, the importance of risk management increases significantly. At this level, success is no longer defined solely by acquiring properties or increasing cash flow—it is defined by your ability to protect what you have built. Advanced investors understand that markets move in cycles, risks evolve over time, and sustainability depends on preparation, discipline, and adaptability. In this chapter, you will learn how to manage risk at a high level, navigate market cycles, and protect your Airbnb portfolio for long-term success.

The first principle of advanced risk management is understanding that risk is dynamic. What appears to be a strong deal today may face challenges in the future due to changes in market conditions, regulations, or competition. This is why successful investors do not rely on static assumptions. Instead, they continuously monitor performance, adjust strategies, and prepare for multiple scenarios. Market cycles play a central role in Airbnb investing. Real estate markets typically move through phases of expansion, peak, contraction, and recovery. During expansion, demand increases, property values rise, and financing becomes more accessible. At the peak, prices may become inflated, and competition intensifies. During contraction, demand may decrease, and property values may decline. Recovery marks the beginning of a new cycle.

Understanding where you are in the market cycle helps you make informed decisions. For example, during expansion, you may focus on growth and acquisition. During contraction, you may prioritize stability, cash flow, and risk reduction. Recognizing these phases allows you to adjust your strategy rather than reacting to changes after they occur.

One of the most important tools for managing risk is maintaining strong DSCR ratios across your portfolio. While lenders may require a minimum DSCR of 1.20, experienced investors aim for higher ratios, such as 1.30 or 1.40. This buffer provides protection against income fluctuations and ensures that your properties can withstand changes in occupancy or pricing.

Another critical factor is leverage. While leverage is a powerful tool for scaling, excessive leverage increases risk. High loan balances and minimal equity can leave you vulnerable during market downturns. Balancing leverage with equity growth is essential for long-term stability. This may involve making larger down payments, refinancing strategically, or paying down debt over time.

Cash reserves are one of the most effective ways to manage risk. Having sufficient reserves allows you to cover expenses during periods of lower income, handle unexpected repairs, and take advantage of new opportunities. Advanced investors often maintain reserves equivalent to six to twelve months of expenses across their portfolio.

Diversification is another key strategy. Relying on a single market or property type increases exposure to localized risks. By investing in multiple markets and property types, you can reduce the impact of downturns in any one area. For example, a coastal vacation market may perform differently than an urban business market. Diversification creates balance and resilience.

Regulatory risk remains one of the most significant challenges in Airbnb investing. Local governments may introduce new restrictions, licensing requirements, or taxes that impact short-term rental operations. Staying informed about regulations and choosing markets with stable policies can reduce this risk. In some cases, having the flexibility to convert properties to long-term rentals provides an additional layer of protection.

Operational risk is another important consideration. Poor management can lead to negative reviews, reduced bookings, and lower income. As your portfolio grows, maintaining consistent quality becomes more challenging. Implementing systems, automation, and quality control measures ensures that your properties continue to perform at a high level.

Insurance and liability protection are also critical components of risk management. Short-term rental properties may require specialized insurance coverage that includes liability protection, property damage, and loss of income. Ensuring that your properties are adequately insured protects you from financial losses and legal exposure.

Economic risk is another factor that cannot be ignored. Changes in the economy can impact travel demand, affecting occupancy and pricing. During economic downturns, discretionary travel may decline, leading to lower income. However, some markets may remain resilient due to essential travel or unique demand drivers. Understanding these dynamics helps you prepare for potential changes.

Interest rate risk is particularly relevant for Airbnb investors using DSCR and Non-QM loans. Rising interest rates can increase borrowing costs, reduce cash flow, and impact refinancing opportunities. Monitoring interest rate trends and structuring loans with flexibility can help mitigate this risk.

Stress testing is an advanced technique used to evaluate how your portfolio performs under different scenarios. This involves analyzing the impact of changes in occupancy, pricing, expenses, and interest rates. By understanding how your properties perform under stress, you can identify weaknesses and take proactive measures to strengthen your portfolio.

Another important concept is liquidity. Real estate is not a liquid asset, meaning it cannot be easily converted to cash. Maintaining access to liquidity through reserves, lines of credit, or refinancing ensures that you can respond to opportunities and challenges. Liquidity provides flexibility and reduces financial pressure during uncertain times.

Portfolio-level analysis is essential for advanced risk management. Instead of focusing on individual properties, you evaluate the performance of your entire portfolio. This includes total cash flow, average DSCR, overall leverage, and diversification. This holistic view allows you to make strategic decisions that enhance stability and growth.

Exit strategies also play a role in risk management. Having multiple exit options—such as selling, refinancing, or converting properties—provides flexibility. This allows you to adapt to changing conditions and protect your investments.

Another advanced strategy is reducing exposure over time. As your portfolio grows, you may choose to pay down debt, sell underperforming properties, or reinvest in lower-risk assets. This gradual shift from growth to preservation helps secure your financial position.

Mental discipline is an often-overlooked aspect of risk management. Emotional decision-making can lead to poor outcomes, especially during market volatility. Successful investors rely on data, systems, and long-term strategy rather than reacting to short-term changes.

Ultimately, advanced risk management is about balance. It is about balancing growth with stability, leverage with equity, and opportunity with caution. By understanding market cycles and implementing strong risk management strategies, you can protect your Airbnb portfolio and ensure long-term success.

Stress Testing and Protecting a Five-Property Airbnb Portfolio

Let's analyze an investor named Mark who owns a portfolio of five Airbnb properties, each valued at $450,000.

Each property has:

- Loan balance: $315,000
- Monthly housing expense: $3,000
- Net operating income: $4,200
- Monthly cash flow: $1,200

Across five properties, Mark's total monthly cash flow is $6,000, or $72,000 annually. His average DSCR is 1.40.

Mark decides to stress test his portfolio.

First, he analyzes a scenario where occupancy drops from 70% to 60%. This reduces net operating income from $4,200 to $3,600 per property.

His new DSCR becomes:

- $3,600 ÷ $3,000 = 1.20

His monthly cash flow per property decreases to $600, and his total portfolio cash flow drops to $3,000 per month.

Next, Mark considers a pricing decline, where ADR decreases by 10%. This reduces net operating income to $3,780 per property.

His DSCR becomes:

- $3,780 ÷ $3,000 = 1.26

His monthly cash flow becomes $780 per property, or $3,900 across the portfolio.

Mark then evaluates a combined scenario where both occupancy and ADR decline. Net operating income drops to $3,200 per property.

His DSCR becomes:

- $3,200 ÷ $3,000 = 1.07

His monthly cash flow drops to $200 per property, or $1,000 across the portfolio.

To prepare for this scenario, Mark maintains reserves of $90,000, equivalent to six months of expenses across all properties.

He also diversifies his portfolio by investing in a different market with stable year-round demand, reducing reliance on a single market.

Additionally, Mark implements dynamic pricing and improves property quality to maintain competitiveness.

Finally, he evaluates refinancing options to reduce interest rates and improve cash flow where possible.

This example demonstrates how stress testing and proactive risk management can protect a portfolio. By understanding potential challenges and preparing for them, Mark ensures that his investments remain stable even under adverse conditions.

As you build and manage your own portfolio, consider how these strategies apply to your situation. Advanced risk management is not about avoiding challenges—it is about being prepared to navigate them successfully.

Chapter 15

From Investor to Owner-Operator – Building a Long-Term Airbnb Business and Legacy

At this final stage of your journey, the conversation shifts from simply acquiring properties and generating income to building something far more powerful—a long-term, sustainable Airbnb business that can operate without your constant involvement and potentially create generational wealth. This chapter is about transformation. It is about evolving from an investor who owns assets into an owner-operator who controls a system, a brand, and a scalable business.

Most investors begin with a transactional mindset. They focus on individual deals, monthly cash flow, and short-term wins. While this approach can produce results, it has limitations. True wealth is not built through isolated transactions—it is built through systems that produce consistent outcomes over time. The goal is to transition from thinking in terms of properties to thinking in terms of a business.

The first step in this transformation is recognizing that your Airbnb portfolio is not just a collection of properties—it is an operating business. Each property is a revenue-generating unit within a larger system. This system includes marketing, pricing, guest experience, operations, financing, and long-term strategy. When these components work together, the result is a business that can grow, adapt, and sustain itself.

Branding becomes increasingly important at this stage. Instead of listing properties individually without connection, you begin to create a cohesive identity. This may include a brand name, consistent design elements, standardized guest experiences, and a recognizable level of quality. A strong brand builds trust, attracts repeat customers, and differentiates your properties in a competitive market.

Customer experience is the foundation of this brand. Guests are not just renting a property—they are experiencing your business. From booking to check-out, every interaction reflects your brand. High-quality communication, clean and well-designed spaces, and thoughtful touches create memorable experiences that lead to positive reviews and repeat bookings. Over time, this consistency becomes a competitive advantage.

At this level, you also begin to think about direct bookings. While platforms like Airbnb provide exposure, they also charge fees and limit your control. Building a direct booking channel—through a website, email list, or social media—allows you to retain more revenue and establish direct relationships with guests. This is a key step in transitioning from platform dependence to business ownership.

Financial systems also evolve. Instead of tracking individual property performance, you begin to analyze your business as a whole. This includes total revenue, operating margins, debt levels, and return on investment across your portfolio. Advanced investors focus on metrics such as net operating margin, portfolio-level DSCR, and capital efficiency.

Another important shift is the role of financing. At the investor level, financing is often viewed as a tool for acquisition. At the business level, financing becomes a strategic lever. You may restructure debt, optimize loan terms, or use financing to support expansion. The goal is to align your financing strategy with your long-term business objectives.

Team building becomes essential as you transition into an owner-operator. A scalable business requires people. This may include property managers, cleaning teams, maintenance staff, virtual assistants, and marketing specialists. Building a reliable team allows you to delegate operational tasks and focus on strategy, growth, and optimization.

Leadership becomes a critical skill. As the owner of a business, your role is to set direction, make decisions, and ensure that your systems are functioning effectively. This requires clear communication, accountability, and the ability to adapt to changing conditions. Strong leadership ensures that your business continues to perform even as it grows.

Another key concept is scalability. A true business is designed to grow without proportional increases in effort. This is achieved through systems, automation, and standardization. Each new property should integrate seamlessly into your existing framework, allowing you to expand without creating chaos.

Technology plays a central role in this transformation. From property management software to dynamic pricing tools, technology enables efficiency and consistency. It allows you to manage multiple properties, automate processes, and analyze performance in real time. Leveraging technology effectively is essential for scaling your business.

Another important aspect is diversification within your business model. This may include expanding into different markets, offering different types of properties, or targeting different guest segments. Diversification reduces risk and creates multiple income streams within your business.

Long-term planning becomes more strategic. Instead of focusing on the next deal, you begin to think in terms of five-year or ten-year goals. This includes decisions about expansion, consolidation, refinancing, and exit strategies. A clear long-term vision guides your actions and ensures that your business evolves in the right direction.

Another advanced concept is monetization beyond rentals. As your brand grows, you may explore additional revenue streams such as consulting, partnerships, or even franchising your model. Your experience and systems become valuable assets that can generate income beyond property ownership.

Legacy building is the final layer of this transformation. Real estate provides an opportunity to create wealth that can be passed down to future generations. Structuring your business in a way that allows for continuity ensures that your efforts have a lasting impact. This may include estate planning, entity structuring, and creating systems that can operate independently of your involvement.

Risk management remains a constant priority. As your business grows, so does your exposure. Maintaining reserves, managing debt, and adapting to market changes ensures that your business remains resilient. The goal is not just growth, but sustainable growth.

Another important consideration is lifestyle design. One of the advantages of building an Airbnb business is the potential for flexibility and freedom. By creating systems and delegating responsibilities, you can design a lifestyle that aligns with your personal goals. This may include more time with family, travel, or pursuing other interests.

Ultimately, the transition from investor to owner-operator is about control. It is about controlling your income, your time, and your future. It is about building a system that works for you rather than relying on individual efforts.

The key takeaway from this chapter is that Airbnb investing is not just a strategy—it is a pathway to building a business. By applying the principles outlined in this book, you can move beyond individual deals and create a scalable, sustainable enterprise that generates long-term wealth.

Transforming a Portfolio into a Scalable Airbnb Business

Let's examine an investor named Anthony who transitions from owning individual Airbnb properties to operating a full-scale business.

Anthony starts with four properties, each generating:

- Gross monthly revenue: $6,000
- Operating expenses: 28% ($1,680)
- Net operating income: $4,320

- Mortgage and fixed costs: $3,000
- Monthly cash flow per property: $1,320

Across four properties, Anthony's total monthly cash flow is $5,280, or $63,360 annually.

At this stage, Anthony is self-managing his properties, spending approximately 30 hours per week on operations.

To transition into a business, Anthony implements systems and hires a team.

He hires a property manager at 10% of revenue, increasing expenses but reducing his workload. His new operating expenses per property become $2,280, reducing net operating income to $3,720.

His new cash flow per property becomes $720, and total monthly cash flow drops to $2,880.

However, Anthony now spends only 10 hours per week managing the business.

With the additional time, Anthony focuses on growth and acquires three more properties.

These new properties benefit from improved systems and generate:

- Gross monthly revenue: $6,500
- Operating expenses: 30% ($1,950)
- Net operating income: $4,550
- Mortgage costs: $3,100
- Cash flow per property: $1,450

With seven properties, Anthony's total monthly cash flow becomes:

- Existing properties: $2,880
- New properties: $4,350
- Total: $7,230 per month

This equals $86,760 annually.

Anthony also builds a direct booking website, reducing platform fees by 5% on 30% of bookings. This increases his net income by approximately $600 per month across the portfolio.

His total monthly cash flow rises to $7,830, or $93,960 annually.

Over time, Anthony's portfolio appreciates, and his total property value reaches $3.5 million. His equity grows significantly, providing opportunities for refinancing and further expansion.

More importantly, Anthony now operates a business rather than managing individual properties. His systems, team, and processes allow him to scale efficiently and focus on strategic growth.

This example demonstrates the transformation from investor to owner-operator. It shows that while short-term cash flow may decrease during the transition, long-term growth and scalability increase significantly.

As you apply these principles, consider how you can build a system that supports your goals. With the right approach, you can create a business that not only generates income but also provides freedom, flexibility, and long-term wealth.

Final Thoughts

Mastery, Momentum, and the Path Forward

As you reach the end of this journey through The Airbnb Mortgage Loan Mastery Series, it is important to pause and recognize what you have built—not just in knowledge, but in perspective. What began as an introduction to Airbnb financing has evolved into a complete framework for acquiring, structuring, scaling, and ultimately transforming real estate investments into a long-term business. You are no longer thinking like a beginner. You are thinking like a strategist, an operator, and an architect of your financial future.

Throughout this series, one principle has remained constant: success in Airbnb investing is not accidental. It is the result of understanding systems, applying strategy, and executing with discipline. Every chapter has reinforced this idea—from learning how DSCR loans work to structuring deals, from scaling portfolios to managing risk, and from optimizing operations to building a business. Each concept builds upon the last, forming a complete ecosystem that supports growth.

At the core of this ecosystem is leverage—not just financial leverage, but strategic leverage. You have learned how to use financing to control assets, how to use data to make decisions, and how to use systems to scale efficiently. These forms of leverage allow you to do more with less, to accelerate your progress, and to create opportunities that would otherwise be out of reach. This is the foundation of modern real estate investing.

But leverage without discipline can lead to instability. That is why risk management has been emphasized throughout this series. Understanding market cycles, maintaining strong DSCR ratios, building reserves, and diversifying your portfolio are not optional—they are essential. They are what allow you to sustain growth over time, to navigate challenges, and to protect what you have built.

Another key theme is adaptability. The Airbnb market is dynamic. Regulations change, competition evolves, and economic conditions shift. The investors who succeed are those who can adapt. They do not rely on a single strategy or a fixed approach. Instead, they remain flexible, continuously learning, adjusting, and improving. This adaptability is what transforms challenges into opportunities.

As you reflect on the strategies covered in this series, it becomes clear that Airbnb investing is not just about properties—it is about systems. It is about creating a repeatable process for finding deals, structuring financing, optimizing performance, and scaling your portfolio. When these systems are in place, your business becomes predictable. It becomes something that you can rely on, something that can grow consistently over time.

The transition from investor to business owner is one of the most significant shifts you can make. It changes how you think, how you operate, and how you measure success. Instead of focusing on individual deals, you begin to focus on the performance of your entire portfolio. Instead of managing tasks, you begin to manage systems. Instead of working in your business, you begin to work on your business.

This shift also opens the door to new possibilities. With a scalable system in place, you can expand into new markets, explore new property types, and create additional revenue streams. You can build a brand, develop partnerships, and even create opportunities beyond real estate. Your business becomes a platform for growth, not just within Airbnb investing, but across multiple areas of your financial life.

One of the most powerful aspects of this journey is the ability to create long-term wealth. Real estate offers a unique combination of cash flow, appreciation, and tax advantages. When combined with strategic financing and disciplined execution, these elements create a compounding effect. Each property contributes to your portfolio, each decision builds momentum, and over time, this momentum becomes transformative.

However, it is important to remember that this is not a race. Building a successful Airbnb business takes time, patience, and consistency. There will be challenges along the way—deals that do not work out, markets that shift, and unexpected obstacles. These experiences are not setbacks; they are part of the process. They provide valuable lessons that strengthen your strategy and improve your decision-making.

Consistency is the key to long-term success. It is not about making one perfect decision, but about making good decisions consistently over time. It is about following your system, maintaining discipline, and staying focused on your goals. This consistency creates stability, builds confidence, and drives results.

Another important aspect of this journey is clarity. Understanding your goals—whether they are financial independence, passive income, or generational wealth—guides your decisions. It helps you determine which opportunities to pursue, which risks to take, and how to structure your portfolio. Clarity ensures that your actions align with your long-term vision.

As you move forward, it is essential to continue learning. The real estate market is constantly evolving, and staying informed allows you to remain competitive. This includes keeping up with market trends, exploring new financing options, and refining your strategies. Continuous learning is what keeps your system effective and your business growing.

Building relationships is another critical component of success. Whether it is lenders, brokers, contractors, or other investors, your network plays a significant role in your journey. Strong relationships provide access to opportunities, support during challenges, and insights that can enhance your strategy. Investing in your network is an investment in your business.

It is also important to celebrate your progress. Each deal you close, each property you acquire, and each milestone you reach is a step forward. Recognizing these achievements reinforces your momentum and keeps you motivated. Success is built one step at a time, and each step matters.

As you look ahead, consider what your next move will be. Perhaps it is acquiring your first property, scaling to your next level, or refining your operations. Whatever it is, approach it with the knowledge, strategy, and confidence that you have developed throughout this series.

The opportunity in Airbnb investing is significant, but it requires action. Knowledge alone is not enough. The value of what you have learned comes from applying it. Taking action, testing your strategies, and refining your approach is what transforms knowledge into results.

Ultimately, this journey is about more than real estate. It is about creating freedom—freedom of time, freedom of income, and freedom of choice. It is about building a system that supports your life, rather than being controlled by it. It is about designing a future that aligns with your goals and values.

As you close this series, remember that you now have the tools to succeed. You understand how to finance Airbnb properties, how to structure deals, how to scale a portfolio, and how to manage risk. You have a framework that can guide your decisions and support your growth.

The path forward is yours to define. Whether you choose to move quickly or take a more gradual approach, the principles remain the same. Stay disciplined, stay adaptable, and stay focused on your goals. With time, effort, and consistency, you can build a portfolio—and a business—that creates lasting value.

This is not the end of your journey. It is the beginning of what comes next.

How to Get a Personalized Airbnb Mortgage Loan Review

If you found *Airbnb Mortgage Loan Fundamentals: How Short-Term Rental Mortgage Loans Work and How to Qualify*, part of *The Airbnb Mortgage Loan Mastery Series*, helpful, you may want to see how these strategies apply to your own financial situation and investment goals. Every investor's profile is unique. Property type, location, projected Airbnb income, credit score, available capital, and lending guidelines all impact what loan programs you may qualify for and how your deal can be structured.

The examples in this book are designed to teach how Airbnb mortgage loans work—but your real options can only be determined by reviewing your specific numbers and investment scenario.

You can request a no-obligation Airbnb mortgage loan consultation here:

Email: info@FinibiMortgage.com

A licensed mortgage professional will review your scenario and explain what Airbnb financing options may be available to you, including DSCR loans, Non-QM programs, and alternative qualification strategies based on your property and financial profile.

No cost. No pressure. No obligation.

Sincerely,

Joseph G. Correa

Licensed Mortgage Loan Originator

Finibi Mortgage Inc.

About the Author

Joseph G. Correa is a licensed mortgage broker and the founder of Finibi Mortgage, a Florida-based brokerage specializing in real estate investment financing, Airbnb and short-term rental loans, and alternative lending strategies for investors, entrepreneurs, and self-employed borrowers. With more than two decades of experience in mortgage lending, underwriting, and financial structuring, Joseph has helped thousands of clients secure funding using intelligent, flexible loan strategies designed for modern real estate investing.

Unlike traditional loan officers who focus only on closing transactions, Joseph's approach is rooted in long-term wealth building. He believes that mortgage financing—especially for Airbnb and investment properties—should be used as a strategic tool to generate cash flow, scale portfolios, and create financial independence. His philosophy centers on using leverage intelligently, allowing investors to grow without relying solely on personal income or traditional lending limitations.

Joseph is widely recognized for his expertise in DSCR loans, Non-QM lending, short-term rental financing, bank statement programs, and creative deal structuring. He specializes in helping investors qualify based on property income rather than personal income, making it possible for beginners, self-employed individuals, and experienced investors to acquire and scale Airbnb portfolios. His ability to simplify complex lending concepts into clear, actionable strategies has empowered countless individuals to enter the real estate market with confidence.

Joseph created *The Airbnb Mortgage Loan Mastery Series* to give investors the same financing knowledge used by banks, private lenders, and institutional real estate operators. His mission is simple: to help people understand how to qualify, structure deals, and scale using modern lending strategies—so they can build profitable Airbnb businesses and long-term wealth.

When he is not structuring deals or writing, Joseph works directly with investors and borrowers across the United States to design customized financing strategies that align with their goals, property types, and growth plans.

The Airbnb Mortgage Loan Mastery Series Roadmap

The Professional Guide to Financing, Scaling, and Profiting from Short-Term Rental Properties

The purpose of *The Airbnb Mortgage Loan Mastery Series* is to give investors the same financing strategies used by banks, lenders, and institutional real estate operators—translated into clear, practical guidance for everyday investors. Each book builds on the last, taking you from foundational knowledge to advanced deal structuring, portfolio scaling, and long-term wealth creation using Airbnb and short-term rental properties.

Book 1 — Airbnb Mortgage Loan Fundamentals This book gives you the foundation. You will understand how Airbnb mortgage loans work, what makes them different from traditional financing, and how lenders evaluate short-term rental properties. You will learn the core concepts of DSCR, Non-QM loans, and income-based qualification, along with who qualifies and how to structure your first deal. Every book that follows builds on this knowledge and shows you how to apply it to real-world investing.

Book 2 — DSCR Airbnb Mortgage Loans This book focuses on one of the most powerful tools in Airbnb investing: DSCR loans. You will learn how to qualify using rental income instead of personal income, how DSCR is calculated using short-term rental data, and how to position your property to meet lender requirements. This book shows you how to break free from traditional income limitations and scale faster.

Book 3 — Airbnb Mortgage Loans for Beginners
This book is designed for first-time investors. You will learn how to buy your first Airbnb property using the right loan strategy, how to analyze deals, and how to overcome common obstacles. It provides a clear, step-by-step path from zero experience to your first successful investment.

Book 4 — Airbnb Investment Property Mortgage Loans This book focuses on scaling. You will learn how to finance multiple Airbnb properties, build a portfolio, and optimize cash flow. It introduces strategies for acquiring properties efficiently and managing them as part of a larger system.

Book 5 — Airbnb Mortgage Loans with No Income Verification

This book explores advanced qualification strategies. You will learn how to get approved without tax returns using DSCR, bank statement, and alternative documentation programs. It is designed for self-employed borrowers and investors who want flexibility in how they qualify.

Book 6 — Luxury Airbnb Mortgage Loans
This book focuses on high-end properties. You will learn how to finance luxury Airbnb investments, analyze high average daily rates, and balance risk with return. It introduces jumbo loan strategies and premium market positioning.

Book 7 — Airbnb Mortgage Loans for Vacation Homes
This book explains how to finance second homes and convert them into profitable short-term rentals. You will learn the difference between second home and investment property guidelines, along with hybrid usage strategies and compliance considerations.

Book 8 — Airbnb Mortgage Loan Refinancing & Cash-Out Strategies
This book teaches you how to unlock equity and scale faster. You will learn how to refinance Airbnb properties, execute cash-out strategies, and recycle capital into new investments.

Book 9 — Airbnb Mortgage Loans for Multi-Unit Properties
This book focuses on duplexes, triplexes, and small multifamily properties. You will learn how to finance multiple income streams within one property, analyze mixed rental models, and navigate zoning and compliance.

Book 10 — Advanced Airbnb Mortgage Loan Structuring

This book brings everything together. You will learn how to combine DSCR, asset-based, and creative financing strategies to close complex deals. It is designed for investors who want to operate at a high level and scale without limits.

This series is designed to be followed step by step or used as a reference based on your current stage. Whether you are just starting or already building a portfolio, each book provides the tools, strategies, and insights needed to move forward with clarity and confidence.

The goal is simple: to help you understand how to finance, structure, and scale Airbnb investments so you can build a profitable, long-term real estate business.

Educational & Financial Disclaimer

This book is provided for educational and informational purposes only. The author and publisher are not engaged in rendering legal, tax, accounting, investment, or financial advice. Although Joseph G. Correa is a licensed mortgage loan originator, the information in this book is intended to provide general education about Airbnb mortgage loans, DSCR financing, and short-term rental investment strategies—not personalized financial, legal, or lending advice.

Mortgage programs, underwriting guidelines, interest rates, credit requirements, and short-term rental financing options vary by lender, investor, state, and economic conditions, and may change at any time without notice. The examples, calculations, and scenarios presented in this book are hypothetical and are for illustration purposes only. They do not represent guaranteed results, loan approvals, or actual investment outcomes.

Short-term rental performance, including Airbnb income, occupancy rates, and average daily rates, is influenced by market demand, competition, seasonality, management quality, and local regulations. These factors can vary significantly and are not guaranteed. Before making any financial decisions—including purchasing an Airbnb property, applying for a DSCR or Non-QM loan, refinancing, or using real estate financing for investment purposes—readers should consult with a qualified mortgage professional, financial advisor, tax advisor, or attorney who can evaluate their specific situation.

Risk Disclosure

Real estate investing and short-term rental financing involve risk. Airbnb properties rely on variable income, which can fluctuate due to changes in demand, competition, economic conditions, and local regulations. There is no guarantee that a property will achieve projected income levels or maintain consistent occupancy.

Borrowing to purchase or refinance investment properties increases financial leverage and risk. Failure to make required mortgage payments could result in foreclosure or loss of property. DSCR and Non-QM loans may carry higher interest rates, stricter terms, or prepayment penalties, which can impact long-term profitability.

Additionally, changes in laws or regulations governing short-term rentals may affect your ability to operate a property as an Airbnb. Investors are responsible for ensuring compliance with all local, state, and federal regulations.

This book teaches structured, strategic, and responsible approaches to Airbnb financing and investing, but no strategy is risk-free. Readers are solely responsible for their financial decisions and outcomes. Neither the author nor the publisher makes any warranties, express or implied, regarding the accuracy, completeness, or applicability of the information in this book to any individual situation.

www.ingramcontent.com/pod-product-compliance
Lightning Source LLC
LaVergne TN
LVHW022221200926
848481LV00006B/2063